LAOCOON.

LAOCOON

An Essay upon the Limits of Painting and Poetry

by GOTTHOLD EPHRAIM LESSING

Translated by *Ellen Frothingham*

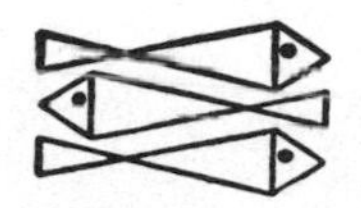

THE NOONDAY PRESS
A DIVISION OF FARRAR, STRAUS
AND GIROUX
NEW YORK

Library of Congress Catalog Card Number: 57-8048

Fifth printing, 1968

MANUFACTURED IN THE UNITED STATES OF AMERICA

PREFACE.

THE first who compared painting with poetry was a man of fine feeling, who was conscious of a similar effect produced on himself by both arts. Both, he perceived, represent absent things as present, give us the appearance as the reality. Both produce illusion, and the illusion of both is pleasing.

A second sought to analyze the nature of this pleasure, and found its source to be in both cases the same. Beauty, our first idea of which is derived from corporeal objects, has universal laws which admit of wide application. They may be extended to actions and thoughts as well as to forms.

A third, pondering upon the value and distribution of these laws, found that some obtained more in painting, others in poetry: that in regard to the latter, therefore, poetry can come to the aid of painting; in regard to the former, painting to the aid of poetry, by illustration and example.

The first was the amateur; the second, the philosopher; the third, the critic.

The first two could not well make a false use of their feeling or their conclusions, whereas with the critic all depends on the right application of his principles in particular cases. And, since there are fifty ingenious critics to one of penetration, it would be a wonder if the application were, in every case, made with the caution indispensable to an exact adjustment of the scales between the two arts.

If Apelles and Protogenes, in their lost works on painting, fixed and illustrated its rules from the already established laws of poetry, we may be sure they did so with the same moderation and exactness with which Aristotle, Cicero, Horace, and Quintilian, in their still existing writings, apply the principles and experiences of painting to eloquence and poetry. It is the prerogative of the ancients in nothing either to exceed or fall short.

But we moderns have in many cases thought to surpass the ancients by transforming their pleasure-paths into highways, though at the risk of reducing the shorter and safer highways to such paths as lead through deserts.

The dazzling antithesis of the Greek Voltaire, that painting is dumb poetry, and poetry speaking painting, stood in no text-book. It was one of those conceits, occurring frequently in Simonides, the inexactness and falsity of which we feel constrained to overlook for the sake of the evident truth they contain.

The ancients, however, did not overlook them. They confined the saying of Simonides to the effect produced by the two arts, not failing to lay stress upon the fact that, notwithstanding the perfect similarity of their effects, the arts themselves differ both in the objects and in the methods of their imitation, ὕλῃ καὶ τρόποις μιμήσεως.

But, as if no such difference existed, many modern critics have drawn the crudest conclusions possible from this agreement between painting and poetry. At one time they confine poetry within the narrower limits of painting, and at another allow painting to fill the whole wide sphere of poetry. Whatever is right in one must be permitted to the other; whatever pleases or displeases in one is necessarily pleasing or displeasing in the other. Full of this idea they, with great assurance, give utterance to the shallowest judgments, whenever they find that poet and painter have treated the same subject in a different way. Such variations they take to be faults, and charge them on painter or poet, according as their taste more inclines to the one art or the other.

This fault-finding criticism has partially misled the virtuosos themselves. In poetry, a fondness for description, and in painting, a fancy for allegory, has arisen from the desire to make the one a speaking picture without really knowing what it can and ought to paint, and the other a dumb poem, without having considered in how far painting can express universal ideas without abandoning its proper sphere and degenerating into an arbitrary method of writing.

To combat that false taste and those ill-grounded criticisms is the chief object of the following chapters. Their origin was accidental, and in their growth they have rather followed the course of my reading than been systematically developed from general principles. They are, therefore, not so much a book as irregular *collectanea* for one.

Yet I flatter myself that, even in this form, they will not be wholly without value. We

Germans suffer from no lack of systematic books. No nation in the world surpasses us in the faculty of deducing from a couple of definitions whatever conclusions we please, in most fair and logical order.

Baumgarten acknowledged that he was indebted to Gesner's dictionary for a large proportion of the examples in his "Æsthetics." If my reasoning be less close than that of Baumgarten, my examples will, at least, savor more of the fountain.

Since I made the Laocoon my point of departure, and return to it more than once in the course of my essay, I wished him to have a share in the title-page. Other slight digressions on various points in the history of ancient art, contribute less to the general design of my work, and have been retained only because I never can hope to find a better place for them.

Further, I would state that, under the name of painting, I include the plastic arts generally; as, under that of poetry, I may have allowed myself sometimes to embrace those other arts, whose imitation is progressive.

LAOCOON.

I.

THE chief and universal characteristic of the Greek masterpieces in painting and sculpture consists, according to Winkelmann, in a noble simplicity and quiet grandeur, both of attitude and expression. "As the depths of the sea," he says,[1] "remain always at rest, however the surface may be agitated, so the expression in the figures of the Greeks reveals in the midst of passion a great and steadfast soul."

"Such a soul is depicted in the countenance of the Laocoon, under sufferings the most intense. Nor is it depicted in the countenance only: the agony betrayed in every nerve and muscle, — we almost fancy we could detect it in the painful contraction of the abdomen alone, without looking at the face and other parts of the body, — this agony, I say, is yet expressed with no violence in the face and attitude. He raises no terrible cry, as Virgil sings of his Laocoon. This would not be possible, from the opening of the mouth, which denotes

[1] Von der Nachahmung der griechischen Werke in der Malerei und Bildhauerkunst, p. 21, 22.

rather an anxious and oppressed sigh, as described by Sadolet. Bodily anguish and moral greatness are diffused in equal measure through the whole structure of the figure; being, as it were, balanced against each other. Laocoon suffers, but he suffers like the Philoctetes of Sophocles. His sufferings pierce us to the soul, but we are tempted to envy the great man his power of endurance."

"To express so noble a soul far outruns the constructive art of natural beauty. The artist must have felt within himself the mental greatness which he has impressed upon his marble. Greece united in one person artist and philosopher, and had more than one Metrodorus. Wisdom joined hands with art and inspired its figures with more than ordinary souls."

The remark which lies at the root of this criticism — that suffering is not expressed in the countenance of Laocoon with the intensity which its violence would lead us to expect — is perfectly just. That this very point, where a shallow observer would judge the artist to have fallen short of nature and not to have attained the true pathos of suffering, furnishes the clearest proof of his wisdom, is also unquestionable. But in the reason which Winkelmann assigns for this wisdom, and the universality of the rule which he deduces from it, I venture to differ from him.

His depreciatory allusion to Virgil was, I confess, the first thing that aroused my doubts, and the second was his comparison of Laocoon with Philoctetes. Using these as my starting-points, I shall proceed to write down my thoughts in the order in which they have occurred to me.

"Laocoon suffers like the Philoctetes of Sophocles." How does Philoctetes suffer? Strange that his sufferings have left such different impressions upon our minds. The complaints, the screams, the wild imprecations with which his pain filled the camp, interrupting the sacrifices and all offices of religion, resounded not less terribly through the desert island to which they had been the cause of his banishment. Nor did the poet hesitate to make the theatre ring with the imitation of these tones of rage, pain, and despair.

The third act of this play has been regarded as much shorter than the others. A proof, say the critics,[1] that the ancients attached little importance to the equal length of the acts. I agree with their conclusion, but should choose some other example in support of it. The cries of pain, the moans, the broken exclamations, *ἆ, ἆ! φεῦ! ἀτταταῖ! ὤ μοὶ, μοί!* the *παπαῖ, παπαῖ!* filling whole lines, of which this act is made up, would naturally require to be prolonged in the delivery and interrupted by more frequent pauses than a connected discourse. In the representation, therefore, this third act must have occupied about as much time as the others. It seems shorter on paper to the reader than it did to the spectator in the theatre.

A cry is the natural expression of bodily pain.

[1] Brumoy Théât. des Grecs, T. ii. p. 89.

Homer's wounded heroes not infrequently fall with a cry to the ground. Venus screams aloud[1] at a scratch, not as being the tender goddess of love, but because suffering nature will have its rights. Even the iron Mars, on feeling the lance of Diomedes, bellows as frightfully as if ten thousand raging warriors were roaring at once, and fills both armies with terror.[2]

High as Homer exalts his heroes in other respects above human nature, they yet remain true to it in their sensitiveness to pain and injuries and in the expression of their feelings by cries or tears or revilings. Judged by their deeds they are creatures of a higher order; in their feelings they are genuine human beings.

We finer Europeans of a wiser posterity have, I know, more control over our lips and eyes. Courtesy and decency forbid cries and tears. We have exchanged the active bravery of the first rude ages for a passive courage. Yet even our ancestors were greater in the latter than the former. But our ancestors were barbarians. To stifle all signs of pain, to meet the stroke of death with unaverted eye, to die laughing under the adder's sting, to weep neither over our own sins nor at the loss of the dearest of friends, are traits of the old northern heroism.[3] The law given by Palnatoko to the Jomsburghers was to fear nothing, nor even to name the word fear.

[1] Iliad v. 343. Ἡ δὲ μέγα ἰάχουσα.

[2] Iliad v. 859.

[3] Th. Bartholinus. De Causis contemptæ a Danis adhuc Gentilibus Mortis, cap. I.

Not so the Greek. He felt and feared. He expressed his pain and his grief. He was ashamed of no human weakness, yet allowed none to hold him back from the pursuit of honor or the performance of a duty. Principle wrought in him what savageness and hardness developed in the barbarian. Greek heroism was like the spark hidden in the pebble, which sleeps till roused by some outward force, and takes from the stone neither clearness nor coldness. The heroism of the barbarian was a bright, devouring flame, ever raging, and blackening, if not consuming, every other good quality.

When Homer makes the Trojans advance to battle with wild cries, while the Greeks march in resolute silence, the commentators very justly observe that the poet means by this distinction to characterize the one as an army of barbarians, the other of civilized men. I am surprised they have not perceived a similar characteristic difference in another passage.[1]

The opposing armies have agreed upon an armistice, and are occupied, not without hot tears on both sides (δάκρυα θερμὰ χέοντες), with the burning of their dead. But Priam forbids his Trojans to weep (οὐδ' εἴα κλαίειν Πρίαμος μέγας), "and for this reason," says Madame Dacier; "he feared they might become too tender-hearted, and return with less spirit to the morrow's fight." Good; but I would ask why Priam alone should apprehend this. Why

[1] Iliad vii. 421.

does not Agamemnon issue the same command to his Greeks? The poet has a deeper meaning. He would show us that only the civilized Greek can weep and yet be brave, while the uncivilized Trojan, to be brave, must stifle all humanity. I am in no wise ashamed to weep (*Νεμεσσῶμαί γε μὲν οὐδὲν κλάιειν*), he elsewhere[1] makes the prudent son of wise Nestor say.

It is worthy of notice that, among the few tragedies which have come down to us from antiquity, there should be two in which bodily pain constitutes not the least part of the hero's misfortunes. Besides Philoctetes we have the dying Hercules, whom also Sophocles represents as wailing, moaning, weeping, and screaming. Thanks to our well-mannered neighbors, those masters of propriety, a whimpering Philoctetes or a screaming Hercules would now be ridiculous and not tolerated upon the stage. One of their latest poets,[2] indeed, has ventured upon a Philoctetes, but he seems not to have dared to show him in his true character.

Among the lost works of Sophocles was a Laocoon. If fate had but spared it to us! From the slight references to the piece in some of the old grammarians, we cannot determine how the poet treated his subject. Of one thing I am convinced,—that he would not have made his Laocoon more of a Stoic than Philoctetes and Hercules. Every thing stoical is untheatrical. Our sympathy is always proportionate with the suffering expressed by the

[1] Odyssey iv. 195. [2] Chateaubrun.

object of our interest. If we behold him bearing his misery with magnanimity, our admiration is excited; but admiration is a cold sentiment, wherein barren wonder excludes not only every warmer emotion, but all vivid personal conception of the suffering.

I come now to my conclusion. If it be true that a cry, as an expression of bodily pain, is not inconsistent with nobility of soul, especially according to the views of the ancient Greeks, then the desire to represent such a soul cannot be the reason why the artist has refused to imitate this cry in his marble. He must have had some other reason for deviating in this respect from his rival, the poet, who expresses it with deliberate intention.

II.

Be it truth or fable that Love made the first attempt in the imitative arts, thus much is certain: that she never tired of guiding the hand of the great masters of antiquity. For although painting, as the art which reproduces objects upon flat surfaces, is now practised in the broadest sense of that definition, yet the wise Greek set much narrower bounds to it. He confined it strictly to the imitation of beauty. The Greek artist represented nothing that was not beautiful. Even the vulgarly beautiful, the beauty of inferior types, he copied only incidentally for practice or recreation. The perfection of the subject must charm in his work. He was too great to require the beholders to be satisfied with the mere barren pleasure arising from a successful likeness or from consideration of the artist's skill. Nothing in his art was dearer to him or seemed to him more noble than the ends of art.

"Who would want to paint you when no one wants to look at you?" says an old epigrammatist[1] to a misshapen man. Many a modern artist would say, "No matter how misshapen you are, I will paint you. Though people may not like to look at you, they will be glad to look at my picture; not as a portrait

[1] See Appendix, note 1.

of you, but as a proof of my skill in making so close a copy of such a monster."

The fondness for making a display with mere manual dexterity, ennobled by no worth in the subject, is too natural not to have produced among the Greeks a Pauson and a Pyreicus. They had such painters, but meted out to them strict justice. Pauson, who confined himself to the beauties of ordinary nature, and whose depraved taste liked best to represent the imperfections and deformities of humanity,[1] lived in the most abandoned poverty;[2] and Pyreicus, who painted barbers' rooms, dirty workshops, donkeys, and kitchen herbs, with all the diligence of a Dutch painter, as if such things were rare or attractive in nature, acquired the surname of Rhyparographer,[3] the dirt-painter. The rich voluptuaries, indeed, paid for his works their weight in gold as if by this fictitious valuation to atone for their insignificance.

Even the magistrates considered this subject a matter worthy their attention, and confined the artist by force within his proper sphere. The law of the Thebans commanding him to make his copies more beautiful than the originals, and never under pain of punishment less so, is well known. This was no law against bunglers, as has been supposed by critics generally, and even by Junius himself,[4]

[1] See Appendix, note 2.
[2] Aristophanes, Plut. v. 602 et Acharnens. v. 854.
[3] Plinius, lib. xxx. sect. 37.
[4] De Pictura vet. lib. ii. cap. iv. sect. 1.

but was aimed against the Greek Ghezzi, and con demned the unworthy artifice of obtaining a likeness by exaggerating the deformities of the model. It was, in fact, a law against caricature.

From this same conception of the beautiful came the law of the Olympic judges. Every conqueror in the Olympic games received a statue, but a portrait-statue was erected only to him who had been thrice victor.[1] Too many indifferent portraits were not allowed among works of art. For although a portrait admits of being idealized, yet the likeness should predominate. It is the ideal of a particular person, not the ideal of humanity.

We laugh when we read that the very arts among the ancients were subject to the control of civil law; but we have no right to laugh. Laws should unquestionably usurp no sway over science, for the object of science is truth. Truth is a necessity of the soul, and to put any restraint upon the gratification of this essential want is tyranny. The object of art, on the contrary, is pleasure, and pleasure is not indispensable. What kind and what degree of pleasure shall be permitted may justly depend on the law-giver.

The plastic arts especially, besides the inevitable influence which they exercise on the character of a nation, have power to work one effect which demands the careful attention of the law. Beautiful statues fashioned from beautiful men reacted upon their creators, and the state was indebted for its beautiful

[1] Plinius, lib. xxxiv. sect. 9.

men to beautiful statues. With us the susceptible imagination of the mother seems to express itself only in monsters.

From this point of view I think I detect a truth in certain old stories which have been rejected as fables. The mothers of Aristomenês, of Aristodamas, of Alexander the Great, Scipio, Augustus, and Galerius, each dreamed during pregnancy that she was visited by a serpent. The serpent was an emblem of divinity.[1] Without it Bacchus, Apollo, Mercury, and Hercules were seldom represented in their beautiful pictures and statues. These honorable women had been feasting their eyes upon the god during the day, and the bewildering dream suggested to them the image of the snake. Thus I vindicate the dream, and show up the explanation given by the pride of their sons and by unblushing flattery. For there must have been some reason for the adulterous fancy always taking the form of a serpent.

But I am wandering from my purpose, which was simply to prove that among the ancients beauty was the supreme law of the imitative arts. This being established, it follows necessarily that whatever else these arts may aim at must give way completely if incompatible with beauty, and, if compatible, must at least be secondary to it.

I will confine myself wholly to expression. There are passions and degrees of passion whose expression produces the most hideous contortions of the face, and throws the whole body into such unnatural

[1] See Appendix, note 3.

positions as to destroy all the beautiful lines that mark it when in a state of greater repose. These passions the old artists either refrained altogether from representing, or softened into emotions which were capable of being expressed with some degree of beauty.

Rage and despair disfigured none of their works. I venture to maintain that they never represented a fury.[1] Wrath they tempered into severity. In poetry we have the wrathful Jupiter, who hurls the thunderbolt; in art he is simply the austere.

Anguish was softened into sadness. Where that was impossible, and where the representation of intense grief would belittle as well as disfigure, how did Timanthes manage? There is a well-known picture by him of the sacrifice of Iphigenia, wherein he gives to the countenance of every spectator a fitting degree of sadness, but veils the face of the father, on which should have been depicted the most intense suffering. This has been the subject of many petty criticisms. "The artist," says one,[2] "had so exhausted himself in representations of sadness that he despaired of depicting the father's face worthily." "He hereby confessed," says another,[3] "that the bitterness of extreme grief cannot

[1] See Appendix, note 4.

[2] Plinius, lib. xxxv. sect. 35. Cum mœstos pinxisset omnes, præcipue patruum, et tristitiæ omnem imaginem consumpsisset, patris ipsius vultum velavit, quem digne non poterat ostendere.

[3] Valerius Maximus, lib. viii. cap. 2. Summi mœroris acerbitatem arte exprimi non posse confessus est.

be expressed by art." I, for my part, see in this no proof of incapacity in the artist or his art. In proportion to the intensity of feeling, the expression of the features is intensified, and nothing is easier than to express extremes. But Timanthes knew the limits which the graces have imposed upon his art. He knew that the grief befitting Agamemnon, as father, produces contortions which are essentially ugly. He carried expression as far as was consistent with beauty and dignity. Ugliness he would gladly have passed over, or have softened, but since his subject admitted of neither, there was nothing left him but to veil it. What he might not paint he left to be imagined. That concealment was in short a sacrifice to beauty; an example to show, not how expression can be carried beyond the limits of art, but how it should be subjected to the first law of art, the law of beauty.

Apply this to the Laocoon and we have the cause we were seeking. The master was striving to attain the greatest beauty under the given conditions of bodily pain. Pain, in its disfiguring extreme, was not compatible with beauty, and must therefore be softened. Screams must be reduced to sighs, not because screams would betray weakness, but because they would deform the countenance to a repulsive degree. Imagine Laocoon's mouth open, and judge. Let him scream, and see. It was, before, a figure to inspire compassion in its beauty and suffering. Now it is ugly, abhorrent, and we gladly avert our eyes from a painful spectacle, destitute of the beauty which alone could turn our pain into the sweet feeling of pity for the suffering object.

The simple opening of the mouth, apart from the violent and repulsive contortions it causes in the other parts of the face, is a blot on a painting and a cavity in a statue productive of the worst possible effect. Montfaucon showed little taste when he pronounced the bearded face of an old man with wide open mouth, to be a Jupiter delivering an oracle.[1] Cannot a god foretell the future without screaming? Would a more becoming posture of the lips cast suspicion upon his prophecies? Valerius cannot make me believe that Ajax was painted screaming in the above-mentioned picture of Timanthes.[2] Far inferior masters, after the decline of art, do not in a single instance make the wildest barbarian open his mouth to scream, even though in mortal terror of his enemy's sword.[3]

This softening of the extremity of bodily suffering into a lesser degree of pain is apparent in the works of many of the old artists. Hercules, writhing in his poisoned robe, from the hand of an unknown master, was not the Hercules of Sophocles, who made the Locrian rocks and the Eubœan promontory ring with his horrid cries. He was gloomy rather than wild.[4] The Philoctetes of Pythagoras Leontinus seemed to communicate his pain to the beholder,

[1] Antiquit. expl. T. i. p. 50.
[2] See Appendix, note 5.
[3] Bellorii Admiranda, Tab. 11, 12.
[4] Plinius, lib. xxxiv. sect. 19.

an effect which would have been destroyed by the slightest disfigurement of the features. It may be asked how I know that this master made a statue of Philoctetes. From a passage in Pliny, which ought not to have waited for my emendation, so evident is the alteration or mutilation it has under gone.[1]

[1] See Appendix, note 6.

III.

But, as already observed, the realm of art has in modern times been greatly enlarged. Its imitations are allowed to extend over all visible nature, of which beauty constitutes but a small part. Truth and expression are taken as its first law. As nature always sacrifices beauty to higher ends, so should the artist subordinate it to his general purpose, and not pursue it further than truth and expression allow. Enough that truth and expression convert what is unsightly in nature into a beauty of art.

Allowing this idea to pass unchallenged at present for whatever it is worth, are there not other independent considerations which should set bounds to expression, and prevent the artist from choosing for his imitation the culminating point of any action?

The single moment of time to which art must confine itself, will lead us, I think, to such considerations. Since the artist can use but a single moment of ever-changing nature, and the painter must further confine his study of this one moment to a single point of view, while their works are made not simply to be looked at, but to be contemplated long and often, evidently the most fruitful moment and the most fruitful aspect of that moment must be chosen. Now that only is fruitful which allows free play to the imagination. The more we see the more we must be able to imagine; and the more we imagine, the more we must think we see. But no moment in the whole course of an action is so disadvantageous in this respect as that of its culmination. There is nothing beyond, and to present the uttermost to the eye is to bind the wings of Fancy, and compel her, since she cannot soar beyond the impression made on the senses, to employ herself with feebler images, shunning as her limit the visible fulness already expressed. When, for instance, Laocoon sighs, imagination can hear him cry; but if he cry, imagination can neither mount a step higher, nor fall a step lower, without seeing him in a more endurable, and therefore less interesting, condition. We hear him merely groaning, or we see him already dead.

Again, since this single moment receives from art an unchanging duration, it should express nothing essentially transitory. All phenomena, whose nature it is suddenly to break out and as suddenly to disappear, which can remain as they are but for a moment; all such phenomena, whether agreeable or otherwise, acquire through the perpetuity conferred upon them by art such an unnatural appearance, that the impression they produce becomes weaker with every fresh observation, till the whole subject at last wearies or disgusts us. La Mettrie, who had himself painted and engraved as a second Democritus, laughs only the first time we look at him. Looked at again, the philosopher becomes a buffoon, and his laugh a grimace. So it is with a cry. Pain, which is so violent as to extort a scream, either soon abates or it must destroy the sufferer. Again, if a man of firmness and endurance cry, he does not do so unceasingly, and only this apparent continuity in art makes the cry degenerate into womanish weakness or childish impatience. This, at least, the sculptor of the Laocoon had to guard against, even had a cry not been an offence against beauty, and were suffering without beauty a legitimate subject of art.

Among the old painters Timomachus seems to have been the one most fond of choosing extremes for his subject. His raving Ajax and infanticide Medea were famous. But from the descriptions we have of them it is clear that he had rare skill in selecting that point which leads the observer to imagine the crisis without actually showing it, and in uniting with this an appearance not so essentially transitory as to become offensive through the continuity conferred by art. He did not paint Medea at the moment of her actually murdering her children, but just before, when motherly love is still struggling with jealousy. We anticipate the result and tremble at the idea of soon seeing Medea in her unmitigated ferocity, our imagination far outstripping any thing the painter could have shown us of that terrible moment. For that reason her prolonged indecision, so far from displeasing us, makes us wish it had been continued in reality. We wish this conflict of passions had never been decided or had lasted at least till time and reflection had weakened her fury and secured the victory to the maternal sentiments. This wisdom on the part of Timomachus won for him great and frequent praise, and raised him far above another artist unknown, who was foolish enough to paint Medea at the height of her madness, thus giving to this transient access of passion a duration that outrages nature. The poet[1] censures him for this, and says very justly, apostrophizing the picture, "Art thou then for ever thirsting for the blood of thy children? Is there always a new Jason and a new Creusa to inflame thy rage? To the devil with the very picture of thee!" he adds angrily.

Of Timomachus' treatment of the raving Ajax, we can judge by what Philostratus tells us.[2] Ajax was not represented at the moment when, raging among the herds, he captures and slays goats and oxen, mistaking them for men. The master showed him sitting weary after these crazy deeds of heroism, and meditating self-destruction. That was really the raving Ajax, not because he is raving at the moment, but because we see that he has been raving, and with what violence his present reaction of shame and despair vividly portrays. We see the force of the tempest in the wrecks and corpses with which it has strewn the beach.

1 Philippus, Anthol. lib. iv. cap. 9, ep. 10.

'Αιεὶ γὰρ διψᾷς βρέφεων φονον. ἠ τις 'Ιήσων
Δεύτερος, ἤ Γλαύκη τις πάλι σοὶ πρόφασις;
'Ερρε καὶ ἐν κηρῷ παιδοκτόνε . . .

2 Vita Apoll. lib. ii. cap. 22.

IV.

A REVIEW of the reasons here alleged for the moderation observed by the sculptor of the Laocoon in the expression of bodily pain, shows them to lie wholly in the peculiar object of his art and its necessary limitations. Scarce one of them would be applicable to poetry.

Without inquiring here how far the poet can succeed in describing physical beauty, so much at least is clear, that since the whole infinite realm of perfection lies open for his imitation, this visible covering under which perfection becomes beauty will be one of his least significant means of interesting us in his characters. Indeed, he often neglects it altogether, feeling sure that if his hero have gained our favor, his nobler qualities will either so engross us that we shall not think of his body, or have so won us that, if we think of it, we shall naturally attribute to him a beautiful, or, at least, no unsightly one. Least of all will he have reference to the eye in every detail not especially addressed to the sense of sight. When Virgil's Laocoon screams, who stops to think that a scream necessitates an open mouth, and that an open mouth is ugly? Enough that "clamores horrendos ad sidera tollit" is fine to the ear, no matter what its effect on the eye. Whoever requires a beautiful picture has missed the whole intention of the poet.

Further, nothing obliges the poet to concentrate his picture into a single moment. He can take up every action, if he will, from its origin, and carry it through all possible changes to its issue. Every change, which would require from the painter a separate picture, costs him but a single touch; a touch, perhaps, which, taken by itself, might offend the imagination, but which, anticipated, as it has been, by what preceded, and softened and atoned for by what follows, loses its individual effect in the admirable result of the whole. Thus were it really unbecoming in a man to cry out in the extremity of bodily pain, how can this momentary weakness lower in our estimation a character whose virtues have previously won our regard? Virgil's Laocoon cries; but this screaming Laocoon is the same we know and love as the most far-seeing of patriots and the tenderest of fathers. We do not attribute the cry to his character, but solely to his intolerable sufferings. We hear in it only those, nor could they have been made sensible to us in any other way.

Who blames the poet, then? Rather must we acknowledge that he was right in introducing the cry, as the sculptor was in omitting it.

But Virgil's is a narrative poem. Would the dramatic poet be included in this justification? A very different impression is made by the mention of a cry and the cry itself. The drama, being meant for a living picture to the spectator, should there fore perhaps conform more strictly to the laws of material painting. In the drama we not only fancy we see and hear a crying Philoctetes, we actually do see and hear him. The more nearly the actor approaches nature, the more sensibly must our eyes and ears be offended, as in nature they undoubtedly are when we hear such loud and violent expressions of pain. Besides, physical suffering in general possesses in a less degree than other evils the power of arousing sympathy. The imagination cannot take hold of it sufficiently for the mere sight to arouse in us any corresponding emotion. Sophocles, therefore, might easily have overstepped the bounds not only of conventional propriety, but of a propriety grounded in the very nature of our sensibilities, in letting Philoctetes and Hercules moan and weep, scream and roar. The by-standers cannot possibly feel such concern for their suffering as these excessive outbreaks seem to demand. To us spectators the lookers-on will seem comparatively cold; and yet we cannot but regard their sympathy as the measure of our own. Add to this that the actor can rarely or never carry the representation of bodily pain to the point of illusion, and perhaps the modern dramatic poets are rather to be praised than blamed for either avoiding this danger altogether or skirting it at a safe distance.

Much would in theory appear unanswerable if the achievements of genius had not proved the contrary. These observations are not without good foundation.

yet in spite of them Philoctetes remains one of the masterpieces of the stage. For a portion of our strictures do not apply to Sophocles, and by a disregard of others he has attained to beauties which the timid critic, but for this example, would never have dreamed of. The following remarks will make this apparent: —

1. The poet has contrived wonderfully to intensify and ennoble the idea of physical pain. He chose a wound, — for we may consider the details of the story dependent upon his choice, in so far as he chose the subject for their sake, — he chose, I say, a wound and not an inward distemper, because the most painful sickness fails to impress us as vividly as an outward hurt. The inward sympathetic fire which consumed Meleager when his mother sacrificed him in the brand to her sisterly fury, would therefore be less dramatic than a wound. This wound, moreover, was a divine punishment. In it a fiercer than any natural poison raged unceasingly, and at appointed intervals an access of ntenser pain occurred, always followed by a heavy sleep, wherein exhausted nature acquired the needed strength for entering again upon the same course of pain. Chateaubrun represents him as wounded simply by the poisoned arrow of a Trojan. But so common an accident gives small scope for extraordinary results. Every one was exposed to it in the old wars; why were the consequences so terrible only in the case of Philoctetes? A natural poison that should work for nine years without destroying

life is far more improbable than all the fabulous miraculous elements with which the Greek decked out his tale.

2. But great and terrible as he made the physical sufferings of his hero, he was well aware that these alone would not suffice to excite any sensible degree of sympathy. He joined with them, therefore, other evils, also insufficient of themselves to move us greatly, but receiving from this connection a darker hue of tragedy, which in turn reacted upon the bodily pain. These evils were complete loss of human companionship, hunger, and all the discomforts attendant on exposure to an inclement sky when thus bereft.[1] Imagine a man under these circumstances, but in possession of health, strength, and industry, and we have a Robinson Crusoe, who has little claim to our compassion, though we are by no means indifferent to his fate. For we are seldom so thoroughly content with human society as not to find a certain charm in thinking of the repose to be enjoyed without its pale; more particularly as every one flatters himself with the idea of being able gradually to dispense altogether with the help of others. Again, imagine a man suffering from the most painful of incurable maladies, but surrounded by kind friends who let him want for nothing, who relieve his pain by all the means in their power, and are always ready to listen to his groans and complaints; we should pity him undoubtedly, but our compassion would soon be exhausted. We should

[1] See Appendix, note 7.

presently shrug our shoulders and counsel patience. Only when all these ills unite in one person, when to solitude is added physical infirmity, when the sick man not only cannot help himself, but has no one to help him, and his groans die away on the desert air, — then we see a wretch afflicted by all the ills to which human nature is exposed, and the very thought of putting ourselves in his place for a moment fills us with horror. We see before us despair in its most dreadful shape, and no compassion is stronger or more melting than that connected with the idea of despair. Such we feel for Philoctetes, especially at the moment when, robbed of his bow, he loses the only means left him of supporting his miserable existence. Alas for the Frenchman who had not the sense to perceive this nor the heart to feel it! or, if he had, was petty enough to sacrifice it all to the pitiful taste of his nation! Chateaubrun gives Philoctetes companionship by introducing a princess into his desert island. Neither is she alone, but has with her a lady of honor: a thing apparently as much needed by the poet as by the princess. All the admirable play with the bow he has left out and introduced in its stead the play of bright eyes. The heroic youth of France would in truth have made themselves very merry over a bow and arrows, whereas nothing is more serious to them than the displeasure of bright eyes. The Greek harrows us with fear lest the wretched Philoctetes should be forced to remain on the island without his bow, and there miserably perish. The Frenchman found a surer way to our hearts by making us fear that the son of Achilles would have to depart without his princess. And this is called by the Parisian critics triumphing over the ancients. One of them even proposed to name Chateaubrun's piece "La difficulté vaincue." [1]

3. Turning now from the effect of the whole, let us examine the separate scenes wherein Philoctetes is no longer the forsaken sufferer, but has hope of leaving the dreary island and returning to his kingdom. His ills are therefore now confined entirely to his painful wound. He moans, he cries, he goes through the most hideous contortions. Against this scene objections on the score of offended propriety may with most reason be brought. They come from an Englishman, a man, therefore, not readily to be suspected of false delicacy. As already hinted, he supports his objections by very good arguments. "All feelings and passions," he says, "with which others can have little sympathy, become offensive if too violently expressed." [2] "It is for the same reason that to cry out with bodily pain, how intolerable soever, appears always unmanly and unbecoming. There is, however, a good deal of sympathy even with bodily pain. If I see a stroke aimed and just ready to fall upon the leg or arm of another person, I naturally shriek and draw back my own leg or my own arm; and when it does fall, I feel it in some measure and am hurt by it as well as the

[1] Mercure de France, April, 1755, p. 177.

[2] "The Theory of Moral Sentiments," by Adam Smith, part i. sect. 2, chap. 1. (London, 1761.)

sufferer. My hurt, however, is no doubt excessively slight, and, upon that account, if he makes any violent outcry, as I cannot go along with him, I never fail to despise him."

Nothing is more deceptive than the laying down of general laws for our emotions. Their web is so fine and intricate that the most cautious speculation is hardly able to take up a single thread and trace it through all its interlacings. And if it could, what should we gain? There is in nature no single, unmixed emotion. With every one spring up a thousand others, the most insignificant of which essentially modifies the original one, so that exception after exception arises until our supposed universal law shrinks into a mere personal experience in a few individual cases. We despise a man, says the Englishman, whom we hear crying out under bodily pain. But not always; not the first time; not when we see that the sufferer does all in his power to suppress expressions of pain; not when we know him to be otherwise a man of resolution. still less when we see him giving proof of firmness in the midst of his suffering; when we see that pain, though it extort a cry, can extort nothing further; that he submits to a continuance of the anguish rather than yield a jot of his opinions or resolves, although such a concession would end his woes. All this we find in Philoctetes. To the old Greek mind moral greatness consisted in unchanging love of friends as well as unfaltering hatred of enemies. This greatness Philoctetes preserves through all his tortures. His own griefs have not so exhausted his tears that he has none to shed over the fate of his old friends. His sufferings have not so enervated him that, to be free from them, he would forgive his enemies and lend himself to their selfish ends. And did this man of rock deserve to be despised by the Athenians, because the waves, that could not shake him, wrung from him a moan?

I confess to having little taste for the philosophy of Cicero in general, but particularly distasteful to me are his views with regard to the endurance of bodily pain set forth in the second book of his Tusculan Disputations. One would suppose, from his abhorrence of all expressions of bodily pain, that he was training a gladiator. He seems to see in such expressions only impatience, not considering that they are often wholly involuntary, and that true courage can be shown in none but voluntary actions. In the play of Sophocles he hears only the cries and complaints of Philoctetes and overlooks altogether his otherwise resolute bearing. Else what excuse for his rhetorical outbreak against the poets? "They would make us effeminate by introducing the bravest of their warriors as complaining." They should complain, for the theatre is no arena. The condemned or hired gladiator was bound to do and bear with grace. No sound of lamentation must be heard, no painful contortion seen. His wounds and death were to amuse the spectators, and art must therefore teach the suppression of all feeling. The least manifestation of it might have aroused compassion, and compassion often excited would soon have put an end to the cruel shows. But what is to be avoided in the arena is the very object of the tragic stage, and here, therefore, demeanor of exactly the opposite kind is required. The heroes on the stage must show feeling, must express their sufferings, and give free course to nature. Any appearance of art and constraint represses sympathy. Boxers in buskin can at most excite our admiration. This term may fitly be applied to the so-called Senecan tragedies. I am convinced that the gladiatorial shows were the chief reason why the Romans never attained even to mediocrity in their tragedies. In the bloody amphitheatre the spectators lost all acquaintance with nature. A Ctesias might have studied his art there, never a Sophocles. The greatest tragic genius, accustomed to these artificial death scenes, could not help degenerating into bombast and rodomontade. But as these were incapable of inspiring true heroism, so were the complaints of Philoctetes incapable of producing effeminacy. The complaints are human, while the deeds are heroic. Both together make the human hero, who is neither effeminate nor callous, but appears first the one and then the other, as now Nature sways him, and now principle and duty triumph. This is the highest type that wisdom can create and art imitate.

4. Sophocles, not content with securing his suffering Philoctetes against contempt, has even shielded him beforehand from such hostile criticism as that employed by the Englishman. Though we may not

always despise a man who cries out under bodily pain, we certainly do not feel that degree of sympathy with him which his cry seems to demand. How then should those comport themselves who are about this screaming Philoctetes? Should they appear to be greatly moved? That were contrary to nature. Should they seem as cold and embarrassed as the by-stander on such occasions is apt actually to be? Such a want of harmony would offend the spectator. Sophocles, as I have said, anticipated this and guarded against it in the following way, — he gave to each of the by-standers a subject of personal interest. They are not solely occupied with Philoctetes and his cries. The attention of the spectator, therefore, is directed to the change wrought in each person's own views and designs by the sympathy excited in him, whether strong or weak, not to the disproportion between the sympathy itself and its exciting cause. Neoptolemus and the chorus have deceived the unhappy Philoctetes, and while perceiving the despair they are bringing upon him they behold him overpowered by one of his accesses of pain. Even should this arouse no great degree of sympathy in them, it must at least lead them to self-examination and prevent their increasing by treachery a misery which they cannot but respect. This the spectator looks for; nor is his expectation disappointed by the magnanimous Neoptolemus. Had Philoctetes been master of his suffering, Neoptolemus would have persevered in his deceit. Philoctetes, deprived by pain of all power of dissimulation, necessary as that seems to prevent his future travelling companion from repenting too soon of his promise to take him with him, Philoctetes, by his naturalness, recalls Neoptolemus to nature. The conversion is admirable, and all the more affecting for being brought about by unaided human nature. The Frenchman had recourse again here to the bright eyes. "De mes déguisemens que penserait Sophie?" says the son of Achilles. But I will think no more of this parody.

Sophocles, in "The Trachiniæ," makes use of this same expedient of combining in the by-standers another emotion with the compassion excited by a cry of physical pain. The pain of Hercules has no enervating effect, but drives him to madness. He thirsts for vengeance, and, in his frenzy, has already seized upon Lichas and dashed him in pieces against the rock. The chorus is composed of women who are naturally overpowered with fear and horror. Their terror, and the doubt whether a god will hasten to Hercules' relief, or whether he will fall a victim to his misfortune, make the chief interest of the piece with but a slight tinge of compassion. As soon as the issue has been decided by the oracle, Hercules grows calm, and all other feelings are lost in our admiration of his final decision. But we must not forget, when comparing the suffering Hercules with the suffering Philoctetes, that one is a demi-god, the other but a man. The man is never ashamed to complain; but the demi-god feels shame that his mortal part has so far triumphed over his immortal, that he should weep and groan like a girl.[1] We moderns do not believe in demi-gods, but require our most insignificant hero to feel and act like one.

That an actor can imitate the cries and convulsions of pain so closely as to produce illusion, I neither deny nor affirm. If our actors cannot, I should want to know whether Garrick found it equally impossible; and, if he could not succeed, I should still have the right to assume a degree of perfection in the acting and declamation of the ancients of which we of to-day can form no idea.

[1] Trach. v. 1088, 1089:

ὅστις ὥστε παρθένος
Βέβρυχα κλαίων . . .

V.

SOME critics of antiquity argue that the Laocoon, though a work of Greek art, must date from the time of the emperors, because it was copied from the Laocoon of Virgil. Of the older scholars who have held this opinion I will mention only Bartolomæus Martiani,[1] and of the moderns, Montfaucon.[2] They doubtless found such remarkable agreement between the work of art and the poem that they could not believe the same circumstances, by no means self-suggesting ones, should have occurred by accident to both sculptor and poet. The question then arose to whom the honor of invention belonged, and they assumed the probabilities to be decidedly in favor of the poet.

They appear, however, to have forgotten that a third alternative is possible. The artist may not have copied the poet any more than the poet the

[1] Topographiæ Urbis Romæ, lib. IV. cap. 14. Et quanquam hi (Agesander et Polydorus et Athenodorus Rhodii) ex Virgilii descriptione statuam hanc formavisse videntur, &c.

[2] Suppl. aux Ant. Expliq. T. i. p. 242. Il semble qu'Agésandre, Polydore, et Athénodore, qui en furent les ouvriers, aient travaillé comme à l'envie, pour laisser un monument qui répondait à l'incomparable description qu'a fait Virgile de Laocoon, &c.

artist; but both perhaps drew their material from some older source, which, Macrobius suggests, might have been Pisander.[1] For, while the works of this Greek writer were still in existence, the fact was familiar to every schoolboy that the Roman poet's whole second book, the entire conquest and destruction of Troy, was not so much imitated as literally translated from the older writer. If then Pisander was Virgil's predecessor in the history of Laocoon also, the Greek artists did not need to draw their material from a Latin poet, and this theory of the date of the group loses its support.

If I were forced to maintain the opinion of Martiani and Montfaucon, I should escape from the difficulty in this way. Pisander's poems are lost, and we can never know with certainty how he told the story of Laocoon. Probably, however, he narrated it with the same attendant circumstances of which we still find traces in the Greek authors. Now these do not in the least agree with the version of Virgil, who must have recast the Greek tradition to suit himself. The fate of Laocoon, as he tells it, is quite his own invention, so that the artists, if their representation harmonize with his, may fairly be supposed to have lived after his time, and have used his description as their model.

Quintus Calaber indeed, like Virgil, makes Laocoon express suspicion of the wooden horse; but the wrath of Minerva, which he thereby incurs, is very differently manifested. As the Trojan utters

[1] See Appendix, note 8.

his warning, the earth trembles beneath him, pain and terror fall upon him; a burning pain rages in his eyes; his brain gives way; he raves, he becomes blind. After his blindness, since he still continues to advise the burning of the wooden horse, Minerva sends two terrible dragons, which, however, attack only Laocoon's children. In vain they stretch out their hands to their father. The poor blind man cannot help them. They are torn and mangled, and the serpents glide away into the ground, doing no injury to Laocoon himself. That this was not peculiar to Quintus,[1] but must have been generally accepted, appears from a passage in Lycophron, where these serpents receive the name of "child-eaters."[2]

But if this circumstance were generally accepted among the Greeks, Greek artists would hardly have ventured to depart from it. Or, if they made variations, these would not be likely to be the same as those of a Roman poet, had they not known him and perhaps been especially commissioned to use him as their model. We must insist on this point, I think, if we would uphold Martiani and Montfaucon. Virgil is the first and only one[3] who represents both father and children as devoured by the serpents; the sculptors have done this also, although, as Greeks, they should not; probably, therefore, they did it in consequence of Virgil's example.

[1] Paralip. lib. xii. v. 398–408.

[2] Or rather serpent, for Lycophron mentions but one:

καὶ παιδοβρῶτος πορκέως νήσους διπλᾶς·

[3] See Appendix, note 9.

I am well aware that this probability falls far short of historical certainty. But since I mean to draw no historical conclusions from it, we may be allowed to use it as an hypothesis on which to base our remarks. Let us suppose, then, that the sculptors used Virgil as their model, and see in what way they would have copied him. The cry has been already discussed. A further comparison may perhaps lead to not less instructive results.

The idea of coiling the murderous serpents about both father and sons, tying them thus into one knot, is certainly a very happy one, and betrays great picturesqueness of fancy. Whose was it? the poet's or the artist's? Montfaucon thinks it is not to be found in the poem;[1] but, in my opinion, he has not read the passage with sufficient care.

> Illi agmine certo
> Laocoonta petunt, et primum parva duorum
> Corpora natorum serpens amplexus uterque
> Implicat et miseros morsu depascitur artus.
> Post ipsum, auxilio subeuntem et tela ferentem,
> Corripiunt spirisque ligant ingentibus.[2]

The poet has described the serpents as being of a wonderful length. They have wound their coils about the boys and seize the father also (corripiunt)

[1] See Appendix, note 10.

[2] Their destined way they take,
And to Laocoon and his children make;
And first around the tender boys they wind,
Then with their sharpened fangs their limbs and bodies grind.
The wretched father, running to their aid
With pious haste, but vain, they next invade. — DRYDEN.

as he comes to their aid. Owing to their great length they could not in an instant have disengaged themselves from the boys. There must therefore have been a moment when the heads and forward parts of the bodies had attacked the father while the boys were still held imprisoned in the hindmost coils. Such a moment is unavoidable in the progress of the poetic picture; and the poet makes it abundantly manifest, though that was not the time to describe it in detail. A passage in Donatus[1] seems to prove that the old commentators were conscious of it; and there was still less likelihood of its escaping the notice of artists whose trained eye was quick to perceive any thing that could be turned to their advantage.

The poet carefully leaves Laocoon's arms free that he may have the full use of his hands.

> Ille simul manibus tendit divellere nodos.[2]

In this point the artist must necessarily have followed him; for nothing contributes more to the expression of life and motion than the action of the hands. In representations of passion, especially, the most speaking countenance is ineffective without it. Arms fastened close to the body by the serpents' coils would have made the whole group cold and dead. We consequently see them in full activity, both in the main figure and the lesser ones, and most active where for the moment the pain is sharpest.

[1] See Appendix, note 11.

[2] With both his hands he labors at the knots.

With the exception of this freedom of the arms, there was, however, nothing in the poet's manner of coiling the serpents which could be turned to account by the artists. Virgil winds them twice round the body and twice round the neck of Laocoon, and lets their heads tower high above him.

> Bis medium amplexi, bis collo squamea circum
> Terga dati, superant capite et cervicibus altis.[1]

This description satisfies our imagination completely. The noblest parts of the body are compressed to suffocation, and the poison is aimed directly at the face. It furnished, however, no picture for the artist, who would show the physical effects of the poison and the pain. To render these conspicuous, the nobler parts of the body must be left as free as possible, subjected to no outward pressure which would change and weaken the play of the suffering nerves and laboring muscles. The double coils would have concealed the whole trunk and rendered invisible that most expressive contraction of the abdomen. What of the body would be distinguishable above or below or between the coils would have been swollen and compressed, not by inward pain but by outward violence. So many rings about the neck would have destroyed the pyramidal shape of the group which is now pleasing to the eye, while the pointed heads of the serpents projecting far above

[1] Twice round his waist their winding volumes rolled,
And twice about his gasping throat they fold.
The priest thus doubly choked, — their crests divide,
And towering o'er his head in triumph ride. — DRYDEN.

this huge mass, would have been such a violation of the rules of proportion that the effect of the whole would have been made repulsive in the extreme. There have been designers so devoid of perception as to follow the poet implicitly. One example of the hideous result may be found among the illustrations by Francis Cleyn.[1] The old sculptors saw at a glance that their art required a totally different treatment. They transferred all the coils from the trunk and neck to the thighs and feet, parts which might be concealed and compressed without injury to the expression. By this means they also conveyed the idea of arrested flight, and a certain immobility very favorable to the arbitrary continuance of one posture.

I know not how it happens that the critics have passed over in silence this marked difference between the coils in the marble and in the poem. It reveals the wisdom of the artist quite as much as another difference which they all comment upon, though rather by way of excuse than of praise, — the difference in the dress. Virgil's Laocoon is in his priestly robes, while in the group he, as well as his two sons, appears completely naked. Some persons, it is said, find a great incongruity in the fact that a king's son, a priest, should be represented naked when offering a sacrifice. To this the critics answer in all seriousness that it is, to be sure, a violation of usage but that the artists were driven to it from inability to give their figures suitable clothing. Sculp-

[1] See Appendix, note 12.

ture, they say, cannot imitate stuffs. Thick folds produce a bad effect. Of two evils they have therefore chosen the lesser, and preferred to offend against truth rather than be necessarily faulty in drapery.[1] The old artists might have laughed at the objection, but I know not what they would have said to this manner of answering it. No greater insult could be paid to art. Suppose sculpture could imitate different textures as well as painting, would Laocoon necessarily have been draped? Should we lose nothing by drapery? Has a garment, the work of slavish hands, as much beauty as an organized body, the work of eternal wisdom? Does the imitation of the one require the same skill, involve the same merit, bring the same honor as the imitation of the other? Do our eyes require but to be deceived, and is it a matter of indifference to them with what they are deceived?

In poetry a robe is no robe. It conceals nothing. Our imagination sees through it in every part. Whether Virgil's Laocoon be clothed or not, the agony in every fibre of his body is equally visible. The brow is bound with the priestly fillet, but not concealed. Nay, so far from being a hinderance, the fillet rather strengthens our impression of the sufferer's agony.

> Perfusus sanie vittas atroque veneno.[2]

His priestly dignity avails him nothing. The very

[1] See Appendix, note 13.

[2] His holy fillets the blue venom blots. — DRYDEN.

badge of it, which wins him universal consideration and respect, is saturated and desecrated with the poisonous slaver.

But this subordinate idea the artist had to sacrifice to the general effect. Had he retained even the fillet, his work would have lost in expression from the partial concealment of the brow which is the seat of expression. As in the case of the cry he sacrificed expression to beauty, he here sacrificed conventionality to expression. Conventionality, indeed, was held of small account among the ancients. They felt that art, in the attainment of beauty, its true end, could dispense with conventionalities altogether. Necessity invented clothes, but what has art to do with necessity? There is a beauty of drapery, I admit; but it is nothing as compared with the beauty of the human form. Will he who can attain to the greater rest content with the lesser? I fear that the most accomplished master in drapery, by his very dexterity, proves his weakness.

VI.

My supposition that the artists imitated the poet is no disparagement to them. On the contrary the manner of their imitation reflects the greatest credit on their wisdom. They followed the poet without suffering him in the smallest particular to mislead them. A model was set them, but the task of transferring it from one art into another gave them abundant opportunity for independent thought. The originality manifested in their deviations from the model proves them to have been no less great in their art than the poet was in his.

Now, reversing the matter, I will suppose the poet to be working after the model set him by the artists. This is a supposition maintained by various scholars.[1] I know of no historical arguments in favor of their opinion. The work appeared to them of such exceeding beauty that they could not believe it to be of comparatively recent date. It must have been made when art was at its perfection, because it was worthy of that period.

We have seen that, admirable as Virgil's picture is, there are yet traits in it unavailable for the

[1] See Appendix, note 14.

artist. The saying therefore requires some modification, that a good poetical description must make a good picture, and that a poet describes well only in so far as his details may be used by the artist. Even without the proof furnished by examples, we should be inclined to predicate such limitation from a consideration of the wider sphere of poetry, the infinite range of our imagination, and the intangibility of its images. These may stand side by side in the greatest number and variety without concealment or detriment to any, just as the objects themselves or their natural symbols would in the narrow limits of time or space.

But if the smaller cannot contain the greater it can be contained in the greater. In other words, if not every trait employed by the descriptive poet can produce an equally good effect on canvas or in marble, can every trait of the artist be equally effective in the work of the poet? Undoubtedly; for what pleases us in a work of art pleases not the eye, but the imagination through the eye. The same picture, whether presented to the imagination by arbitrary or natural signs, must always give us a similar pleasure, though not always in the same degree.

But even granting this, I confess that the idea of Virgil's having imitated the artists is more inconceivable to me than the contrary hypothesis. If the artists copied the poet, I can account for all their deviations. Differences would necessarily have arisen, because many traits employed by him with good effect would in their work have been objectionable. But why such deviations in the poet? Would he not have given us an admirable picture by copying the group faithfully in every particular?[1]

I can perfectly understand how his fancy, working independently, should have suggested to him this and that feature, but I see no reason why his judgment should have thought it necessary to transform the beauties that were before his eyes into these differing ones.

It even seems to me that, had Virgil used this group as his model, he could hardly have contented himself with leaving the general embrace of the three bodies within the serpents' folds to be thus guessed at. The impression upon his eye would have been so vivid and admirable, that he could not have failed to give the position greater prominence in his description. As I have said, that was not the time to dwell upon its details; but the addition of a single word might have put a decisive emphasis upon it, even in the shadow in which the poet was constrained to leave it. What the artist could present without that word, the poet would not have failed to express by it, had the work of art been before him.

The artist had imperative reasons for not allowing the sufferings of his Laocoon to break out into cries. But if the poet had had before him in the marble this touching union of pain with beauty, he would certainly have been under no necessity of disregard-

[1] See Appendix, note 15.

ing the idea of manly dignity and magnanimous patience arising from it and making his Laocoon suddenly startle us with that terrible cry. Richardson says that Virgil's Laocoon needed to scream, because the poet's object was not so much to excite compassion for him as to arouse fear and horror among the Trojans. This I am ready to grant, although Richardson appears not to have considered that the poet is not giving the description in his own person, but puts it into the mouth of Æneas, who, in his narration to Dido, spared no pains to arouse her compassion. The cry, however, is not what surprises me, but the absence of all intermediate stages of emotion, which the marble could not have failed to suggest to the poet if, as we are supposing, he had used that as his model. Richardson goes on to say, that the story of Laocoon was meant only as an introduction to the pathetic description of the final destruction of Troy, and that the poet was therefore anxious not to divert to the misfortunes of a private citizen the attention which should be concentrated on the last dreadful night of a great city.[1] But this is a painter's point of view, and here inadmissible. In the poem, the fate of Laocoon and the destruction of the city do not stand side by side as in a picture. They form no single whole to be embraced at one glance, in which case alone there would have been danger of having the eye more attracted by the Laocoon than by the burning city. The two descriptions succeed each other, and I fail to see

[1] See Appendix, note 16.

how the deepest emotion produced by the first could prejudice the one that follows. Any want of effect in the second must be owing to its inherent want of pathos.

Still less reason would the poet have had for altering the serpents' coils. In the marble they occupy the hands and encumber the feet, an arrangement not less impressive to the imagination than satisfactory to the eye. The picture is so distinct and clear that words can scarcely make it plainer than natural signs.

> Micat alter et ipsum
> Laocoonta petit, totumque infraque supraque
> Implicat et rabido tandem ferit ilia morsu.
> . . . . . .
> At serpens lapsu crebro redeunte subintrat
> Lubricus, intortoque ligat genua infima nodo.

These lines are by Sadolet. They would doubtless have come with greater picturesqueness from Virgil, had his fancy been fired by the visible model. Under those circumstances he would certainly have written better lines than those we now have of him.

> Bis medium amplexi, bis collo squamea circum
> Terga dati, superant capite et cervicibus altis.

These details satisfy the imagination, it is true; but not if we dwell upon them and try to bring them distinctly before us. We must look now at the serpents, and now at Laocoon. The moment we try to combine them into one picture, the grouping begins to displease, and appear in the highest degree unpicturesque.

But these deviations from his supposed model, even if not unfortunate, were entirely arbitrary. Imitation is intended to produce likeness, but how can likeness result from needless changes? Such changes rather show that the intention was not to produce likeness, consequently that there has been no imitation.

Perhaps not of the whole, some may urge, but of certain parts. Good; but what are the parts so exactly corresponding in the marble and in the poem, that the poet might seem to have borrowed them from the sculptor? The father, the children, and the serpents, both poet and sculptor received from history. Except what is traditional in both, they agree in nothing but the single circumstance that father and sons are bound by the serpents' coils into a single knot. But this arose from the new version, according to which father and sons were involved in a common destruction,—a version, as already shown, to be attributed rather to Virgil, since the Greek traditions tell the story differently. If, then, there should have been any imitation here, it is more likely to have been on the side of the artist than of the poet. In all other respects their representations differ, but in such a way that the deviations, if made by the artist, are perfectly consistent with an intention to copy the poet, being such as the sphere and limitations of his art would impose on him. They are, on the contrary, so many arguments against the supposed imitation of the sculptor by the poet. Those who, in the face of these objections, still maintain this supposition, can only mean that the group is older than the poem.

VII.

When we speak of an artist as imitating a poet or a poet an artist, we may mean one of two things,—either that one makes the work of the other his actual model, or that the same original is before them both, and one borrows from the other the manner of copying it.

When Virgil describes the shield of Æneas, his imitation of the artist who made the shield is of the former kind. The work of art, not what it represents, is his model. Even if he describe the devices upon it they are described as part of the shield, not as independently existing objects. Had Virgil, on the other hand, copied the group of the Laocoon, this would have been an imitation of the second kind. He would then have been copying, not the actual group, but what the group represents, and would have borrowed from the marble only the details of his copy.

In imitations of the first kind the poet is an originator, in those of the second a copyist. The first is part of the universal imitation which constitutes the very essence of his art, and his work is that of a genius, whether his model be nature or the product of other arts. The second degrades him utterly

Instead of the thing itself, he imitates its imitations, and gives us a lifeless reflection of another's genius for original touches of his own.

In the by no means rare cases where poet and artist must study their common original from the same point of view, their copies cannot but coincide in many respects, although there may have been no manner of imitation or emulation between them. These coincidences among contemporaneous artists and poets may lead to mutual illustrations of things no longer present to us. But to try to help out these illustrations by tracing design where was only chance, and especially by attributing to the poet at every detail a reference to this statue or that picture, is doing him very doubtful service. Nor is the reader a gainer by a process which renders the beautiful passages perfectly intelligible, no doubt, but at the sacrifice of all their life.

This is the design and the mistake of a famous English work by the Rev. Mr. Spence, entitled, "Polymetis; or, An inquiry concerning the agreement between the works of the Roman poets and the remains of the ancient artists, being an attempt to illustrate them mutually from one another."[1] Spence has brought to his work great classical learning and a thorough knowledge of the surviving works of ancient art. His design of using these as means to explain the Roman poets, and making the poets in turn throw light on works of art hitherto

[1] The first edition was issued in 1747; the second, 1755. Selections by N. Tindal have been printed more than once.

imperfectly understood, has been in many instances happily accomplished. But I nevertheless maintain that to every reader of taste his book must be intolerable.

When Valerius Flaccus describes the winged thunderbolts on the shields of the Roman soldiers, —

> Nec primus radios, miles Romane, corusci
> Fulminis et rutilas scutis diffuderis alas,

the description is naturally made more intelligible to me by seeing the representation of such a shield on an ancient monument.[1] It is possible that the old armorers represented Mars upon helmets and shields in the same hovering attitude that Addison thought he saw him in with Rhea on an ancient coin,[2] and that Juvenal had such a helmet or shield in mind in that allusion of his which, till Addison, had been a puzzle to all commentators.

The passage in Ovid where the wearied Cephalus invokes Aura, the cooling zephyr, —

> "Aura . . . . . venias . . . .
> Meque juves, intresque sinus, gratissima, nostros,"

and his Procris takes this Aura for the name of a rival, — this passage, I confess, seems to me more natural when I see that the ancients in their works of art personified the gentle breezes, and, under the name Auræ, worshipped certain female sylphs.[3]

I acknowledge that when Juvenal compares an idle patrician to a Hermes-column, we should hardly

[1] Val. Flaccus, lib. vi. v. 55, 56. Polymetis, dial. vi. p. 50.
[2] See Appendix, note 17. [3] See Appendix, note 18.

perceive the point of the comparison unless we had seen such a column and knew it to be a poorly cut pillar, bearing the head, or at most the trunk, of the god, and, owing to the want of hands and feet, suggesting the idea of inactivity.[1]

Illustrations of this kind are not to be despised, though neither always necessary nor always conclusive. Either the poet regarded the work of art not as a copy but as an independent original, or both artist and poet were embodying certain accepted ideas. Their representations would necessarily have many points of resemblance, which serve as so many proofs of the universality of the ideas.

But when Tibullus describes Apollo as he appeared to him in a dream, — the fairest of youths, his temples wreathed with the chaste laurel, Syrian odors breathing from his golden hair that falls in ripples over his long neck, his whole body as pink and white as the cheek of the bride when led to her bridegroom, — why need these traits have been borrowed from famous old pictures? Echion's "nova nupta verecundia notabilis" may have been in Rome and been copied thousands of times: did that prove virgin modesty itself to have vanished from the world? Since the painter saw it, was no poet to see it more save in the painter's imitation?[2] Or when another poet speaks of Vulcan as wearied and his face reddened by the forge, did he need a picture to

[1] See Appendix, note 19.

[2] Tibullus, Eleg. 4, lib. iii. Polymetis, dial. viii.

teach him that labor wearies and heat reddens?[1] Or when Lucretius describes the alternations of the seasons and brings them before us in the order of nature, with their whole train of effects on earth and air, was Lucretius the creature of a day? had he lived through no entire year and seen its changes, that he must needs have taken his description from a procession of statues representing the seasons? Did he need to learn from statues the old poetic device of making actual beings out of such abstractions?[2] Or Virgil's "pontem indignatus Araxes," that admirable poetic picture of a river overflowing its banks and tearing down the bridge that spans it,— do we not destroy all its beauty by making it simply a reference to some work of art, wherein the river god was represented as actually demolishing a bridge?[3] What do we want of such illustrations which banish the poet from his own clearest lines to give us in his place the reflection of some artist's fancy?

I regret that this tasteless conceit of substituting for the creations of the poet's own imagination a familiarity with those of others should have rendered a book, so useful as the Polymetis might have been made, as offensive as the feeblest commentaries of the shallowest quibblers, and far more derogatory to the classic authors. Still more do I regret that Addison should in this respect have been the predecessor of Spence, and, in his praiseworthy

[1] Statius, lib. i. Sylv. 5, v. 8. Polymetis, dial. viii.

[2] See Appendix, note 20.

[3] Æneid, lib. viii. 725. Polymetis, dial. xiv.

desire to make the old works of art serve as interpreters, have failed to discriminate between those cases where imitation of the artist would be becoming in the poet, and those where it would be degrading to him.[1]

[1] In various passages of his Travels [Remarks on Italy' and his Dialogues on Ancient Medals.

VIII.

Spence has the strangest notions of the resemblance between painting and poetry. He believes the two arts to have been so closely connected among the ancients that they always went hand in hand, the poet never losing sight of the painter, nor the painter of the poet. That poetry has the wider sphere, that beauties are within her reach which painting can never attain, that she may often see reason to prefer unpicturesque beauties to picturesque ones, — these things seem never to have occurred to him. The slightest difference, therefore, between the old poets and artists throws him into an embarrassment from which it taxes all his ingenuity to escape.

The poets generally gave Bacchus horns. Spence is therefore surprised that we seldom see these appendages on his statues.[1] He suggests one reason and another; now the ignorance of the antiquarians, and again "the smallness of the horns themselves, which were very likely to be hid under the crown of grapes or ivy which is almost a constant ornament of the head of Bacchus." He goes all round the true cause without ever suspecting it. The horns of Bacchus were not a natural growth

[1] Polymetis, dial. ix.

like those of fauns and satyrs. They were ornaments which he could assume or lay aside at pleasure.

> Tibi, cum sine cornibus adstas,
> Virgineum caput est, . . .

says Ovid in his solemn invocation to Bacchus.[1] He could therefore show himself without horns, and did, in fact, thus show himself when he wished to appear in his virgin beauty. In this form artists would choose to represent him, and necessarily omitted all disagreeable accompaniments. Horns fastened to the diadem, as we see them on a head in the royal museum in Berlin,[2] would have been a cumbersome appendage, as would also the diadem itself, concealing the beautiful brow. For this reason the diadem appears as rarely as the horns on the statues of Bacchus, although, as its inventor, he is often crowned with it by the poets. In poetry both horns and diadem served as subtle allusions to the deeds and character of the god: in a picture or statue they would have stood in the way of greater beauties. If Bacchus, as I believe, received the name of Biformis, *Δίμορφος*, from having an aspect of beauty as well as of terror, the artists would naturally have chosen the shape best adapted to the object of their art.

In the Roman poets Minerva and Juno often

[1] Metamorph. lib. iv. 19, 20. When thou appearest unhorned, thy head is as the head of a virgin.

[2] Begeri Thes. Brandenb. vol. iii. p. 242.

hurl the thunderbolt. Why are they not so represented in art? asks Spence.[1] He answers, "This power was the privilege of these two goddesses, the reason of which was, perhaps, first learnt in the Samothracian mysteries. But since, among the ancient Romans, artists were considered as of inferior rank, and therefore rarely initiated into them, they would doubtless know nothing of them; and what they knew not of they clearly could not represent." I should like to ask Spence whether these common people were working independently, or under the orders of superiors who might be initiated into the mysteries; whether the artists occupied such a degraded position among the Greeks; whether the Roman artists were not for the most part Greeks by birth; and so on.

Statius and Valerius Flaccus describe an angry Venus with such terrible features that we should take her at the moment for a fury rather than for the goddess of love. Spence searches in vain for such a Venus among the works of ancient art. What is his conclusion? That more is allowed to the poet than to the sculptor and painter? That should have been his inference. But he has once for all established as a general rule that "scarce any thing can be good in a poetical description which would appear absurd if represented in a statue or picture."[2] Consequently the poets must be wrong. "Statius and Valerius Flaccus belong to an age when Roman poetry was already in its decline. In this very

[1] Polymetis, dial. vi. [2] Polymetis, dial. xx.

passage they display their bad judgment and corrupted taste. Among the poets of a better age such a repudiation of the laws of artistic expression will never be found."[1]

Such criticism shows small power of discrimination. I do not propose to undertake the defence of either Statius or Valerius, but will simply make a general remark. The gods and other spiritual beings represented by the artist are not precisely the same as those introduced by the poet. To the artist they are personified abstractions which must always be characterized in the same way, or we fail to recognize them. In poetry, on the contrary, they are real beings, acting and working, and possessing, besides their general character, qualities and passions which may upon occasion take precedence. Venus is to the sculptor simply love. He must therefore endow her with all the modest beauty, all the tender charms, which, as delighting us in the beloved object, go to make up our abstract idea of love. The least departure from this ideal prevents our recognizing her image. Beauty distinguished more by majesty than modesty is no longer Venus but Juno. Charms commanding and manly rather than tender, give us, instead of a Venus, a Minerva. A Venus all wrath, a Venus urged by revenge and rage, is to the sculptor a contradiction in terms. For love, as love, never is angry, never avenges itself. To the poet, Venus is love also, but she is the goddess of love, who has her own individuality outside

[1] Polymetis, dial. vii.

of this one characteristic, and can therefore be actuated by aversion as well as affection. What wonder, then, that in poetry she blazes into anger and rage, especially under the provocation of insulted love?

The artist, indeed, like the poet, may, in works composed of several figures, introduce Venus or any other deity, not simply by her one characteristic, but as a living, acting being. But the actions, if not the direct results of her character, must not be at variance with it. Venus delivering to her son the armor of the gods is a subject equally suitable to artist and poet. For here she can be endowed with all the grace and beauty befitting the goddess of love. Such treatment will be of advantage as helping us the more easily to recognize her. But when Venus, intent on revenging herself on her contemners, the men of Lemnos, wild, in colossal shape, with cheeks inflamed and dishevelled hair, seizes the torch, and, wrapping a black robe about her, flies downward on the storm-cloud, — that is no moment for the painter, because he has no means of making us recognize her. The poet alone has the privilege of availing himself of it. He can unite it so closely with some other moment when the goddess is the true Venus, that we do not in the fury forget the goddess of love. Flaccus does this, —

> Neque enim alma videri
> Jam tumet; aut tereti crinem subnectitur auro,
> Sidereos diffusa sinus. Eadem effera et ingens

Et maculis suffecta genas ; pinumque sonantem
Virginibus Stygiis, nigramque simillima pallam.[1]

And Statius also, —

Illa Paphon veterem centumque altaria linquens,
Nec vultu nec crine prior, solvisse jugalem
Ceston, et Idalias procul ablegasse volucres
Fertur. Erant certe, media qui noctis in umbra
Divam, alios ignes majoraque tela gerentem,
Tartarias inter thalamis volitasse sorores
Vulgarent : utque implicitis arcana domorum
Anguibus, et sæva formidine cuncta replerit
Limina.[2]

Or, we may say, the poet alone possesses the art of so combining negative with positive traits as to unite two appearances in one. No longer now the tender Venus, her hair no more confined with golden clasps, no azure draperies floating about her, without her girdle, armed with other flames and larger

[1] Argonaut. lib. ii. v. 102–106. "Gracious the goddess is not emulous to appear, nor does she bind her hair with the burnished gold, letting her starry tresses float about her. Wild she is and huge, her cheeks suffused with spots ; most like to the Stygian virgins with crackling torch and black mantle."

[2] Thebaid. lib. v. 61–64. "Leaving ancient Paphos and the hundred altars, not like her former self in countenance or the fashion of her hair, she is said to have loosened the nuptial girdle and have sent away her doves. Some report that in the dead of night, bearing other fires and mightier arms, she had hasted with the Tartarean sisters to bed-chambers, and filled the secret places of homes with twining snakes, and all thresholds with cruel fear."

arrows, the goddess hastes downward, attended by furies of like aspect with herself. Must the poet abstain from the use of this device because artists are debarred from it? If painting claim to be the sister of poetry, let the younger at least not be jealous of the elder, nor seek to deprive her of ornaments unbecoming to herself.

IX.

WHEN we compare poet and painter in particular instances, we should be careful to inquire whether both have had entire freedom, and been allowed to labor for the highest results of their art without the exercise of any constraint from without.

Religion often exercised such constraint upon the old artists. A work, devotional in character, must often be less perfect than one intended solely to produce pleasure. Superstition loaded the gods with symbols which were not always reverenced in proportion to their beauty.

In the temple of Bacchus at Lemnos, from which the pious Hypsipyle rescued her father under the guise of the deity,[1] the god was represented horned. So he doubtless appeared in all his temples, the horns being symbols typical of his nature and functions. The unfettered artist, whose Bacchus was not designed for a temple, omitted the symbol. If, among the statues of the god that remain to us, we find none with horns,[2] that circumstance perhaps proves that none of them were sacred statues, representing the god in the shape under which he was worshipped. We should naturally expect, too, that

[1] See Appendix, note 21. [2] See Appendix, note 22.

against such the fury of the pious iconoclasts in the first centuries of Christianity would have been especially directed. Only here and there a work of art was spared, because it had never been desecrated by being made an object of worship.

But since, among the antiques that have been unburied, there are specimens of both kinds, we should discriminate and call only those works of art which are the handiwork of the artist, purely as artist, those where he has been able to make beauty his first and last object. All the rest, all that show an evident religious tendency, are unworthy to be called works of art. In them Art was not working for her own sake, but was simply the tool of Religion, having symbolic representations forced upon her with more regard to their significance than their beauty. By this I do not mean to deny that religion often sacrificed meaning to beauty, or so far ceased to emphasize it, out of regard for art and the finer taste of the age, that beauty seemed to have been the sole end in view.

If we make no such distinction, there will be perpetual strife between connoisseurs and antiquarians from their failure to understand each other. When the connoisseur maintains, according to his conception of the end and aim of art, that certain things never could have been made by one of the old artists, meaning never by one working as artist from his own impulse, the antiquarian will understand him to say that they could never have been fashioned by the artist, as workman, under the influence of religion or any other power outside the domain of art. He will therefore think to confute his antagonist by showing some figure which the connoisseur, without hesitation, but to the great vexation of the learned world, will condemn back to the rubbish from which it had been dug.[1]

But there is danger, on the other hand, of exaggerating the influence of religion on art. Spence furnishes a remarkable instance of this. He found in Ovid that Vesta was not worshipped in her temple under any human image, and he thence drew the conclusion that there had never been any statues of the goddess. What had passed for such must be statues, not of Vesta, but of a vestal virgin.[2] An extraordinary conclusion! Because the goddess was worshipped in one of her temples under the symbol of fire, did artists therefore lose all right to personify after their fashion a being to whom the poets give distinct personality, making her the daughter of Saturn and Ops, bringing her into danger of falling under the ill treatment of Priapus, and narrating yet other things in regard to her? For Spence commits the further error of applying to all the temples of Vesta and to her worship generally what Ovid says only of a certain temple at Rome.[3] She was not everywhere worshipped as in this temple at Rome. Until Numa erected this particular sanctuary, she was not so worshipped even in Italy. Numa

[1] See Appendix, note 23.
[2] Polymetis, dial. vii.
[3] See Appendix, note 24.

allowed no deity to be represented in the shape of man or beast. In this prohibition of all personal representations of Vesta consisted, doubtless, the reformation which he introduced into her rites. Ovid himself tells us that, before the time of Numa, there were statues of Vesta in her temple, which, when her priestess Sylvia became a mother, covered their eyes with their virgin hands.[1] Yet further proof that in the temples of the goddess outside the city, in the Roman provinces, her worship was not conducted in the manner prescribed by Numa, is furnished by various old inscriptions, where mention is made of a priest of Vesta (Pontificis Vestæ).[2] At Corinth, again, was a temple of Vesta without statues, having only an altar whereon sacrifices were offered to the goddess.[3] But did the Greeks, therefore, have no statues of Vesta? There was one at Athens in the Prytaneum, next to the statue of Peace.[4] The people of Iasos boasted of having one in the open air, upon which snow and rain never fell.[5] Pliny mentions one in a sitting posture, from the chisel of Scopas, in the Servilian gardens at Rome, in his day.[6] Granting that it is difficult for us now to distinguish between a vestal virgin and the goddess herself, does that prove that the ancients

[1] See Appendix, note 25.

[2] Lipsius de Vesta et Vestalibus, cap. 13.

[3] Pausanias, Corinth. cap. xxxv. p. 198 (edit. Kuhn).

[4] Pausanias, Attic. cap. xviii. p. 41.

[5] Polyb. Hist. lib. xvi. sect. 2, Op. T. ii. p. 443 (edit. Ernest.).

[6] See Appendix, note 26.

were not able or did not care to make the distinction? Certain attributes point evidently more to one than the other. The sceptre, the torch, and the palladium would seem to belong exclusively to the goddess. The tympanum, attributed to her by Codinus, belongs to her, perhaps, only as the Earth. Or perhaps Codinus himself did not know exactly what it was he saw.[1]

[1] See Appendix, note 27.

X.

SPENCE's surprise is again aroused in a way that shows how little he has reflected on the limits of poetry and painting.

"As to the muses in general," he says, "it is remarkable that the poets say but little of them in a descriptive way; much less than might indeed be expected for deities to whom they were so particularly obliged." [1]

What is this but expressing surprise that the poets, when they speak of the muses, do not use the dumb language of the painter? In poetry, Urania is the muse of astronomy. Her name and her employment reveal her office. In art she can be recognized only by the wand with which she points to a globe of the heavens. The wand, the globe, and the attitude are the letters with which the artist spells out for us the name Urania. But when the poet wants to say that Urania had long read her death in the stars,—

> Ipsa diu positis lethum prædixerat astris
> Urania.[2]

Why should he add, out of regard to the artist,— Urania, wand in hand, with the heavenly globe

[1] Polymetis, dial. viii. [2] Statius, Theb. viii. 551.

before her? Would that not be as if a man, with the power and privilege of speech, were to employ the signs which the mutes in a Turkish seraglio had invented to supply the want of a voice?

Spence expresses the same surprise in regard to the moral beings, or those divinities who, among the ancients, presided over the virtues and undertook the guidance of human life.[1] "It is observable," he says, "that the Roman poets say less of the best of these moral beings than might be expected. The artists are much fuller on this head; and one who would know how they were each set off must go to the medals of the Roman emperors. The poets, in fact, speak of them very often as persons; but of their attributes, their dress, and the rest of their figure they generally say but little."

When a poet personifies abstractions he sufficiently indicates their character by their name and employment.

These means are wanting to the artist, who must therefore give to his personified abstractions certain symbols by which they may be recognized. These symbols, because they are something else and mean something else, constitute them allegorical figures.

A female figure holding a bridle in her hand, another leaning against a column, are allegorical beings. But in poetry Temperance and Constancy are not allegorical beings, but personified abstractions.

Necessity invented these symbols for the artist,

[1] Polymetis, dial. x.

who could not otherwise indicate the significance of this or that figure. But why should the poet, for whom no such necessity exists, be obliged to accept the conditions imposed upon the artist?

What excites Spence's surprise should, in fact, be prescribed as a law to all poets. They should not regard the limitations of painting as beauties in their own art, nor consider the expedients which painting has invented in order to keep pace with poetry, as graces which they have any reason to envy her. By the use of symbols the artist exalts a mere figure into a being of a higher order. Should the poet employ the same artistic machinery he would convert a superior being into a doll.

Conformity to this rule was as persistently observed by the ancients as its studious violation is by the viciousness of modern poets. All their imaginary beings go masked, and the writers who have most skill in this masquerade generally understand least the real object of their work, which is to let their personages act, and by their actions reveal their character.

Among the attributes by which the artist individualizes his abstractions, there is one class, however, better adapted to the poet than those we have been considering, and more worthy of his use. I refer to such as are not strictly allegorical, but may be regarded as instruments which the beings bearing them would or could use, should they ever come to act as real persons. The bridle in the hand of Temperance, the pillar which supports Constancy are purely allegorical, and cannot therefore be used by the poet. The scales in the hand of Justice are less so, because the right use of the scales is one of the duties of Justice. The lyre or flute in the hand of a muse, the lance in the hand of Mars, hammer and tongs in the hands of Vulcan, are not symbols at all, but simply instruments without which none of the actions characteristic of these beings could be performed. To this class belong the attributes sometimes woven by the old poets into their descriptions, and which, in distinction from those that are allegorical, I would call the poetical. These signify the thing itself, while the others denote only some thing similar.[1]

[1] See Appendix, note 28.

XI.

COUNT CAYLUS also seems to require that the poet should deck out the creatures of his imagination with allegorical attributes.[1] The Count understood painting better than poetry.

But other points more worthy of remark have struck me in the same work of his, some of the most important of which I shall mention here for closer consideration.

The artist, in the Count's opinion, should make himself better acquainted with Homer, that greatest of all word painters, — that second nature, in fact. He calls attention to the rich and fresh material furnished by the narrative of the great Greek, and assures the painter that the more closely he follows the poet in every detail, the nearer his work will approach to perfection.

This is confounding the two kinds of imitation mentioned above. The painter is not only to copy the same thing that the poet has copied, but he is to copy it with the same touches. He is to use the poet not only as narrator, but as poet.

But why is not this second kind of imitation,

[1] See Appendix, note 29.

which we have found to be degrading to the poet, equally so to the artist? If there had existed previous to Homer such a series of pictures as he suggests to Count Caylus, and we knew that the poet had composed his work from them, would he not lose greatly in our estimation? Why should we not in like manner cease to admire the artist who should do no more than translate the words of the poet into form and color?

The reason I suppose to be this. In art the difficulty appears to lie more in the execution than in the invention, while with poetry the contrary is the case. There the execution seems easy in comparison with the invention. Had Virgil copied the twining of the serpents about Laocoon and his sons from the marble, then his description would lose its chief merit; for what we consider the more difficult part had been done for him. The first conception of this grouping in the imagination is a far greater achievement than the expression of it in words. But if the sculptor have borrowed the grouping from the poet, we still consider him deserving of great praise, although he have not the merit of the first conception. For to give expression in marble is incalculably more difficult than to give it in words. We weigh invention and execution in opposite scales, and are inclined to require from the master as much less of one as he has given us more of the other.

There are even cases where the artist deserves more credit for copying Nature through the medium of the poet's imitation than directly from herself.

The painter who makes a beautiful landscape from the description of a Thomson, does more than one who takes his picture at first hand from nature. The latter sees his model before him; the former must, by an effort of imagination, think he sees it. One makes a beautiful picture from vivid, sensible impressions, the other from the feeble, uncertain representations of arbitrary signs.

From this natural readiness to excuse the artist from the merit of invention, has arisen on his part an equally natural indifference to it. Perceiving that invention could never be his strong point, but that his fame must rest chiefly on execution, he ceased to care whether his theme were new or old, whether it had been used once or a hundred times, belonged to himself or another. He kept within the narrow range of a few subjects, grown familiar to himself and the public, and directed all his invention to the introducing of some change in the treatment, some new combination of the old objects. That is actually the meaning attached to the word "invention" in the old text-books on painting. For although they divide it into the artistic and the poetic, yet even the poetic does not extend to the originating of a subject, but solely to the arrangement or expression.[1] It is invention, not of the whole, but of the individual parts and their connection with one another; invention of that inferior kind which Horace recommended to his tragic poet:

[1] Betrachtungen über die Malerei, p. 159.

> Tuque
> Rectius Iliacum carmen deducis in actus,
> Quam si proferres ignota indictaque primus.[1]

Recommended, I say, but not commanded. He recommended it as easier for him, more convenient, more advantageous: he did not command it as intrinsically nobler and better.

The poet, indeed, has a great advantage when he treats of familiar historical facts and well-known characters. He can omit a hundred tiresome details otherwise indispensable to an understanding of the piece. And the sooner he is understood, the sooner he can interest his readers. The same advantage is possessed by the painter when his subject is so familiar to us that we take in at a glance the meaning and design of his whole composition, and can not only see that his characters are speaking, but can even hear what they say. On that first glance the chief effect depends. If that necessitate a tiresome guessing and pondering, our readiness to be touched is chilled. We take revenge upon the unwise artist by hardening ourselves against his expression; and alas for him, if to that expression he have sacrificed beauty! No inducement remains for us to linger before his work. What we see does not please us, and what it means we do not understand.

Considering now these two points: first, that

[1] Ad Pisones, v. 128–130. "Thou wilt do better to write out in acts the story of Troy, than to tell of things not yet known nor sung."

invention and novelty in the subject are by no means what we chiefly require from the painter; and secondly, that a familiar subject helps and quickens the effect of his art, I think we shall find a deeper reason for his avoidance of new subjects than indolence or ignorance or absorption of his whole industry and time in the mechanical difficulties of his art, which are the causes assigned for it by Count Caylus. We may even be inclined to praise as a wise and, as far as we are concerned, a beneficent forbearance on the part of the artist, what seemed to us at first a deficiency in art and a curtailment of our enjoyment.

I have no fear that experience will contradict me. Painters will be grateful to the Count for his good intentions, but will hardly make as general use of his advice as he expects. Should such, however, be the case, a new Caylus would be needed at the end of a hundred years to remind us of the old themes and recall the artist to a field where others before him have reaped undying laurels. Or shall we expect the public to be as learned as the connoisseur with his books, and familiar with all the scenes of history and fable that offer fit subjects for art? I grant that artists, since the time of Raphael, would have done better to take Homer for their manual than Ovid. But since, once for all, they have not done so, let us leave the public in its old ruts, and not throw more difficulties in the way of its pleasure than are necessary to make the pleasure worth having.

Protogenes had painted the mother of Aristotle. I know not how much the philosopher paid for the picture, but instead of the full payment, or perhaps over and above it, he gave the painter a piece of advice which was of more value than the money. Not, as I believe, in the way of flattery, but because he knew that art needed to make itself universally intelligible, he advised him to paint the exploits of Alexander. The whole world was ringing with the fame of them, and he could foresee that their memory would remain to all posterity. But Protogenes was not wise enough to follow this counsel. "Impetus animi," says Pliny, "et quædam artis libido,"[1] a certain presumption in art, and a craving after something new and strange, led him to the choice of other subjects. He preferred the story of Ialysus,[2] of Cydippe, and others of like kind, whose meaning we can now scarce even conjecture.

[1] Lib. xxxv. sect. 36.

[2] See Appendix, note 30.

XII.

HOMER treats of two different classes of beings and actions, — the visible and the invisible. This distinction cannot be made on canvas, where every thing is visible, and visible in precisely the same way.

When Count Caylus, therefore, makes pictures of invisible actions follow immediately upon pictures of visible ones; and in scenes of mixed actions, participated in by beings of both kinds, does not, and perhaps cannot, indicate how those figures which only we who look at the picture are supposed to see, shall be so represented that the characters in the picture shall not see them, or at least shall not look as if they could not help seeing them, he makes the whole series, as well as many separate pictures, in the highest degree confused, unintelligible, and self-contradictory.

With the book before us this difficulty might finally be overcome. The great objection would be that, with the loss of all distinction to the eye between the visible and the invisible beings, all the characteristic traits must likewise disappear, which serve to elevate the higher order of beings above the lower.

When, for instance, the gods who take different sides in the Trojan war come at last to actual blows, the contest goes on in the poem unseen.[1] This invisibility leaves the imagination free play to enlarge the scene at will, and picture the gods and their movements on a scale far grander than the measure of common humanity. But painting must accept a visible theatre, whose various fixed parts become a scale of measurement for the persons acting upon it. This scale is always before the eye, and the disproportionate size of any superhuman figures makes beings that were grand in the poem monstrous on canvas.

Minerva, on whom Mars had made the first attack, steps backward and with mighty hand lifts from the ground an enormous stone, black and rough, which, in old times, had required the strength of many men to be rolled into its place and set up as a landmark.[2]

ἡ δ' ἀναχασσαμένη λίθον εἵλετο χειρὶ παχείῃ
κείμενον ἐν πεδίῳ, μέλανα, τρηχύν τε μέγαν τε,
τόν ῥ' ἄνδρες πρότεροι θέσαν ἔμμεναι οὖρον ἀρούρης·

To obtain an adequate idea of the size of this stone, we must remember that Homer makes his heroes twice as strong as the mightiest men of his day, yet

[1] Iliad xxi. 385.

[2] She only stepped
Backward a space, and with her powerful hand
Lifted a stone that lay upon the plain,
Black, huge, and jagged, which the men of old
Had placed there for a landmark. — BRYANT.

says they were far surpassed in strength by the men whom Nestor had known in his youth. Now if Minerva is to hurl at Mars a stone which it had required, not one man, but many men of the time of Nestor's youth to set up as a landmark, what, I ask, should be the stature of the goddess? If her size be proportioned to that of the stone, all marvel ceases. A being of thrice my size can, of course, throw three times as large a stone. But if the stature of the goddess be not proportioned to the size of the stone, the result is a palpable improbability in the picture which cannot be atoned for by the cold consideration that a goddess is necessarily of supernatural strength.

Mars, overthrown by this enormous stone, covered seven hides, —

ἑπτὰ δ' ἐπέσχε πέλεθρα πεσών.

It is impossible for the painter to give the god this extraordinary size. Yet if he do not, we have no Homeric Mars lying on the ground, but an ordinary warrior.[1]

Longinus says, it has often seemed to him that Homer's design was to raise his men to gods and degrade his deities to men. Painting accomplishes this. On canvas we lose every thing which in poetry exalts the gods above mere godlike men. Size, strength, speed, — qualities which Homer has always in store for his gods in miraculous measure, far surpassing any thing he attributes to his most

[1] See Appendix, note 31.

famous heroes,[1]—are necessarily reduced in the picture to the common scale of humanity. Jupiter and Agamemnon, Apollo and Achilles, Ajax and Mars, are all kindred beings, only to be distinguished by some arbitrary outward sign.

The expedient to which painters have recourse to indicate that a certain character is supposed to be invisible, is a thin cloud veiling the side of the figure that is turned towards the other actors on the scene. This cloud seems at first to be borrowed from Homer himself. For, when in the confusion of battle one of the chief heroes becomes exposed to a danger from which nothing short of divine aid can save him, the poet makes his guardian deity veil him in a thick cloud or in darkness, and so lead him from the field. Paris is thus delivered by Venus,[2] Idæus by Neptune,[3] Hector by Apollo.[4] Caylus never omits strongly to recommend to the artist this mist or cloud, whenever he is to paint pictures of such occurrences. But who does not perceive that this veiling in mist and darkness is only the poet's way of saying that the hero became invisible? It always seems strange to me, therefore, to find this poetical expression embodied in a picture, and an actual cloud introduced, behind which, as behind a screen, the hero stands hidden from his enemy. This was not the poet's meaning. The artist in this exceeds the limits of painting. His cloud is a hieroglyphic, a purely symbolic sign, which does not

[1] See Appendix, note 32.
[2] Iliad iii. 381.
[3] Iliad v. 23.
[4] Iliad xx. 444.

make the rescued hero invisible, but simply says to the observers,—"You are to suppose this man to be invisible." It is no better than the rolls of paper with sentences upon them, which issue from the mouth of personages in the old Gothic pictures.

Homer, to be sure, makes Achilles give three thrusts with his lance at the thick cloud[1] while Apollo is carrying off Hector,—*τρὶς δ' ἠέρα τύψε βαθεῖαν.* But that, in the language of poetry, only means that Achilles was so enraged that he thrust three times with his lance before perceiving that his enemy was no longer before him. Achilles saw no actual cloud. The whole secret of this invisibility lay not in the cloud, but in the god's swift withdrawal of the imperilled hero. In order to indicate that the withdrawal took place so instantaneously that no human eye could follow the retreating form, the poet begins by throwing over his hero a cloud; not because the by-standers saw the cloud in the place of the vanished shape, but because to our mind things in a cloud are invisible.

The opposite device is sometimes used, and, instead of the object being made invisible, the subject is smitten with blindness. Thus Neptune blinds the eyes of Achilles when he rescues Æneas from his murderous hands by transporting him from the thick of the contest to the rear.[2] In reality, the eyes of Achilles were no more blinded in the one case than in the other the rescued heroes were veiled in a cloud. Both are mere expressions employed by the

[1] Iliad xx. 446. [2] Iliad xx. 321.

poet to impress more vividly on our minds the extreme rapidity of the removal; the disappearance, as we should call it.

But artists have appropriated the Homeric mist not only in those cases of concealment or disappearance where Homer himself employed or would have employed it, but in cases where the spectator was to perceive something which the characters on the canvas, or some of them at least, were not to be conscious of. Minerva was visible to Achilles only, when she restrained him from committing violence against Agamemnon. "I know no other way of expressing this," says Caylus, "than to interpose a cloud between the goddess and the other members of the council." This is entirely contrary to the spirit of the poet. Invisibility was the natural condition of his deities. So far from any stroke of blindness or intercepting of the rays of light being necessary to render them invisible,[1] a special illumination, an increased power of human vision was needed to see them. Not only, therefore, is this cloud an arbitrary and not a natural symbol in painting, but it does not possess the clearness which, as an arbitrary sign, it should. It has a double meaning, being employed as well to make the invisible visible as to render the visible invisible.

[1] See Appendix, note 33.

XIII.

If Homer's works were completely destroyed, and nothing remained of the Iliad and Odyssey but this series of pictures proposed by Caylus, should we from these — even supposing them to be executed by the best masters — form the same idea that we now have of the poet's descriptive talent alone, setting aside all his other qualities as a poet?

Let us take the first piece that comes to hand, — the picture of the plague.[1] What do we see on the canvas? Dead bodies, the flame of funeral pyres, the dying busied with the dead, the angry god upon a cloud discharging his arrows. The profuse wealth of the picture becomes poverty in the poet. Should we attempt to restore the text of Homer from this picture, what can we make him say? "Thereupon the wrath of Apollo was kindled, and he shot his arrows among the Grecian army. Many Greeks died, and their bodies were burned." Now let us turn to Homer himself:[1]

[1] Iliad i. 44–53. Tableaux tirés de l'Iliade, p. 70.

Down he came,
Down from the summit of the Olympian mount,
Wrathful in heart; his shoulders bore the bow
And hollow quiver; there the arrows rang
Upon the shoulders of the angry god,
As on he moved. He came as comes the night,

Ὣς ἔφατ' εὐχόμενος, τοῦ δ' ἔκλυε Φοῖβος Ἀπόλλων,
βῆ δὲ κατ' Οὐλύμποιο καρήνων χωόμενος κῆρ,
τόξ' ὤμοισιν ἔχων ἀμφηρεφέα τε φαρέτρην.
ἔκλαγξαν δ' ἄρ' ὀϊστοὶ ἐπ' ὤμων χωομένοιο,
αὐτοῦ κινηθέντος· ὁ δ' ἤϊε νυκτὶ ἐοικώς.
ἕζετ' ἔπειτ' ἀπάνευθε νεῶν, μετὰ δ' ἰὸν ἕηκεν·
δεινὴ δὲ κλαγγὴ γένετ' ἀργυρέοιο βιοῖο.
οὐρῆας μὲν πρῶτον ἐπῴχετο καὶ κύνας ἀργούς,
αὐτὰρ ἔπειτ' αὐτοῖσι βέλος ἐχεπευκὲς ἐφιείς
βάλλ'· αἰεὶ δὲ πυραὶ νεκύων καίοντο θαμειαί.

The poet here is as far beyond the painter, as life is better than a picture. Wrathful, with bow and quiver, Apollo descends from the Olympian towers. I not only see him, but hear him. At every step the arrows rattle on the shoulders of the angry god. He enters among the host like the night. Now he seats himself over against the ships, and, with a terrible clang of the silver bow, sends his first shaft against the mules and dogs. Next he turns his poisoned darts upon the warriors themselves, and unceasing blaze on every side the corpse-laden pyres. It is impossible to translate into any other language the musical painting heard in the poet's words. Equally impossible would it be to infer it from the canvas. Yet this is the least of the advantages

And, seated from the ships aloof, sent forth
An arrow; terrible was heard the clang
Of that resplendent bow. At first he smote
The mules and the swift dogs, and then on man
He turned the deadly arrow. All around
Glared evermore the frequent funeral piles. — BRYANT.

possessed by the poetical picture. Its chief superiority is that it leads us through a whole gallery of pictures up to the point depicted by the artist.

But the plague is perhaps not a favorable subject for a picture. Take the council of the gods,[1] which is more particularly addressed to the eye. An open palace of gold, groups of the fairest and most majestic forms, goblet in hand, served by eternal youth in the person of Hebe. What architecture! what masses of light and shade! what contrasts! what variety of expression! Where shall I begin, where cease, to feast my eyes? If the painter thus enchant me, how much more will the poet! I open the book and find myself deceived. I read four good, plain lines, which might very appropriately be written under the painting. They contain material for a picture, but are in themselves none.[1]

Οἱ δὲ θεοὶ πὰρ Ζηνὶ καθήμενοι ἠγορόωντο
χρυσέῳ ἐν δαπέδῳ, μετὰ δέ σφισι πότνια Ἥβη
νέκταρ ἐῳνοχόει· τοὶ δὲ χρυσέοις δεπάεσσιν
δειδέχατ' ἀλλήλους, Τρώων πόλιν εἰσορόωντες.

Apollonius, or a more indifferent poet still, would not have said it worse. Here Homer is as far behind the artist as, in the former instance, he surpassed him.

[1] Iliad iv. 1–4. Tableaux tirés de l'Iliade, p. 30.
Meantime the immortal gods with Jupiter
Upon his golden pavement sat and held
A council. Hebe, honored of them all,
Ministered nectar, and from cups of gold
They pledged each other, looking down on Troy.
BRYANT.

Yet, except in these four lines, Caylus finds no single picture in the whole fourth book of the Iliad. "Rich as this book is," he says, "in its manifold exhortations to battle, in the abundance of its conspicuous and contrasting characters, in the skill with which the masses to be set in motion are brought before us, it is yet entirely unavailable for painting." "Rich as it otherwise is," he might have added, "in what are called poetic pictures." For surely in this fourth book we find as many such pictures, and as perfect, as in any of the whole poem. Where is there a more detailed, a more striking picture than that of Pandarus breaking the truce at the instigation of Minerva, and discharging his arrow at Menelaus? than that of the advance of the Grecian army? or of the mutual attack? or of the deed of Ulysses, whereby he avenges the death of his friend Leucus?

What must we conclude, except that not a few of the finest pictures in Homer are no pictures for the artist? that the artist can extract pictures from him where he himself has none? that such of his as the artist can use would be poor indeed did they show us no more than we see on the canvas? what, in short, but a negative answer to my question? Painted pictures drawn from the poems of Homer, however numerous and however admirable they may be, can give us no idea of the descriptive talent of the poet.

XIV.

IF it, then, be true that a poem not in itself picturesque may yet be rich in subjects for an artist, while another in a high degree picturesque may yield him nothing, this puts an end to the theory of Count Caylus, that the test of a poem is its availability for the artist, and that a poet's rank should depend upon the number of pictures he supplies to the painter.[1]

Far be it from us to give this theory even the sanction of our silence. Milton would be the first to fall an innocent victim. Indeed, the contemptuous judgment which Caylus passes upon the English poet would seem to be the result not so much of national taste as of this assumed rule. Milton resembles Homer, he says, in little excepting loss of sight. Milton, it is true, can fill no picture galleries. But if, so long as I retained my bodily eye, its sphere must be the measure of my inward vision, then I should esteem its loss a gain, as freeing me from such limitations.

The fact that "Paradise Lost" furnishes few subjects for a painter no more prevents it from being the greatest epic since Homer, than the story of

[1] See Appendix, note 34.

the passion of Christ becomes a poem, because you can hardly insert the head of a pin in any part of the narrative without touching some passage which has employed a crowd of the greatest artists. The evangelists state their facts with the dryest possible simplicity, and the painter uses their various details while the narrators themselves manifested not the smallest spark of genius for the picturesque. There are picturesque and unpicturesque facts, and the historian may relate the most picturesque without picturesqueness, as the poet can make a picture of those least adapted to the painter's use.

To regard the matter otherwise is to allow ourselves to be misled by the double meaning of a word. A picture in poetry is not necessarily one which can be transferred to canvas. But every touch, or every combination of touches, by means of which the poet brings his subject so vividly before us that we are more conscious of the subject than of his words, is picturesque, and makes what we call a picture; that is, it produces that degree of illusion which a painted picture is peculiarly qualified to excite, and which we in fact most frequently and naturally experience in the contemplation of the painted canvas.[1]

[1] See Appendix, note 35.

XV.

Experience shows that the poet can produce this degree of illusion by the representation of other than visible objects. He therefore has at his command whole classes of subjects which elude the artist. Dryden's "Ode on Cecilia's Day" is full of musical pictures, but gives no employment to the brush. But I will not lose myself in examples of this kind, for they after all teach us little more than that colors are not tones, and ears not eyes.

I will confine myself to pictures of visible objects, available alike to poet and painter. What is the reason that many poetical pictures of this class are unsuitable for the painter, while many painted pictures lose their chief effect in the hands of the poet?

Examples may help us. I revert to the picture of Pandarus in the fourth book of the Iliad, as one of the most detailed and graphic in all Homer. From the seizing of the bow to the flight of the arrow every incident is painted; and each one follows its predecessor so closely, and yet is so distinct from it, that a person who knew nothing of the use of a bow could learn it from this picture alone.[1] Pan-

[1] See Appendix, note 36.

darus brings forth his bow, attaches the string, opens the quiver, selects a well-feathered arrow never before used, adjusts the notch of the arrow to the string, and draws back both string and arrow; the string approaches his breast, the iron point of the arrow nears the bow, the great arched bow springs back with a mighty twang, the cord rings, and away leaps the eager arrow speeding towards the mark.

Caylus cannot have overlooked this admirable picture. What, then, did he find which made him judge it no fitting subject for an artist? And what in the council and carousal of the gods made that seem more adapted to his purpose? The subjects are visible in one case as in the other, and what more does the painter need for his canvas?

The difficulty must be this. Although both themes, as representing visible objects, are equally adapted to painting, there is this essential difference between them: one is a visible progressive action, the various parts of which follow one another in time; the other is a visible stationary action, the development of whose various parts takes place in space. Since painting, because its signs or means of imitation can be combined only in space, must relinquish all representations of time, therefore progressive actions, as such, cannot come within its range. It must content itself with actions in space; in other words, with mere bodies, whose attitude lets us infer their action. Poetry, on the contrary —

XVI.

But I will try to prove my conclusions by starting from first principles.

I argue thus. If it be true that painting employs wholly different signs or means of imitation from poetry, — the one using forms and colors in space, the other articulate sounds in time, — and if signs must unquestionably stand in convenient relation with the thing signified, then signs arranged side by side can represent only objects existing side by side, or whose parts so exist, while consecutive signs can express only objects which succeed each other, or whose parts succeed each other, in time.

Objects which exist side by side, or whose parts so exist, are called bodies. Consequently bodies with their visible properties are the peculiar subjects of painting.

Objects which succeed each other, or whose parts succeed each other in time, are actions. Consequently actions are the peculiar subjects of poetry.

All bodies, however, exist not only in space, but also in time. They continue, and, at any moment of their continuance, may assume a different appearance and stand in different relations. Every one of these momentary appearances and groupings was the result of a preceding, may become the cause of a following, and is therefore the centre of a present, action. Consequently painting can imitate actions also, but only as they are suggested through forms.

Actions, on the other hand, cannot exist independently, but must always be joined to certain agents. In so far as those agents are bodies or are regarded as such, poetry describes also bodies, but only indirectly through actions.

Painting, in its coexistent compositions, can use but a single moment of an action, and must therefore choose the most pregnant one, the one most suggestive of what has gone before and what is to follow.

Poetry, in its progressive imitations, can use but a single attribute of bodies, and must choose that one which gives the most vivid picture of the body as exercised in this particular action.

Hence the rule for the employment of a single descriptive epithet, and the cause of the rare occurrence of descriptions of physical objects.

I should place less confidence in this dry chain of conclusions, did I not find them fully confirmed by Homer, or, rather, had they not been first suggested to me by Homer's method. These principles alone furnish a key to the noble style of the Greek, and enable us to pass just judgment on the opposite method of many modern poets who insist upon emulating the artist in a point where they must of necessity remain inferior to him.

I find that Homer paints nothing but progressive actions. All bodies, all separate objects, are painted only as they take part in such actions, and generally with a single touch. No wonder, then, that artists find in Homer's pictures little or nothing to their purpose, and that their only harvest is where the narration brings together in a space favorable to art a number of beautiful shapes in graceful attitudes, however little the poet himself may have painted shapes, attitudes, or space. If we study one by one the whole series of pictures proposed by Caylus, we shall in every case find proof of the justness of these conclusions.

Here, then, I leave the Count with his desire to make the painter's color-stone the touchstone of the poet, and proceed to examine more closely the style of Homer.

For a single thing, as I have said, Homer has commonly but a single epithet. A ship is to him at one time the black ship, at another the hollow ship, and again the swift ship. At most it is the well-manned black ship. Further painting of the ship he does not attempt. But of the ship's sailing, its departure and arrival, he makes so detailed a picture, that the artist would have to paint five or six, to put the whole upon his canvas.

If circumstances compel Homer to fix our attention for a length of time on any one object, he still makes no picture of it which an artist can follow with his brush. By countless devices he presents this single object in a series of moments, in every one of which it assumes a different form. Only in the final one can the painter seize it, and show us ready made what the artist has been showing us in the making. If Homer, for instance, wants us to see the chariot of Juno, Hebe must put it together piece by piece before our eyes. We see the wheels, the axle, the seat, the pole, the traces and straps, not already in place, but as they come together under Hebe's hands. The wheels are the only part on which the poet bestows more than a single epithet. He shows us separately the eight brazen spokes, the golden fellies, the tires of brass, and the silver nave. It would almost seem that, as there was more than one wheel, he wished to spend as much more time in the description as the putting on would require in reality.[1]

Ἥβη δ' ἀμφ' ὀχέεσσι θοῶς βάλε καμπύλα κύκλα,
χάλκεα ὀκτάκνημα, σιδηρέῳ ἄξονι ἀμφίς.
τῶν ἤτοι χρυσέη ἴτυς ἄφθιτος, αὐτὰρ ὕπερθεν
χάλκε' ἐπίσσωτρα προσαρηρότα, θαῦμα ἰδέσθαι·
πλῆμναι δ' ἀργύρου εἰσὶ περίδρομοι ἀμφοτέρωθεν.
δίφρος δὲ χρυσέοισι καὶ ἀργυρέοισιν ἱμᾶσιν
ἐντέταται, δοιαὶ δὲ περίδρομοι ἄντυγές εἰσιν.

[1] Iliad v. 722.

Hebe rolled the wheels,
Each with eight spokes, and joined them to the ends
Of the steel axle, — fellies wrought of gold,
Bound with a brazen rim to last for ages, —
A wonder to behold. The hollow naves
Were silver, and on gold and silver cords
Was slung the chariot's seat; in silver hooks
Rested the reins; and silver was the pole
Where the fair yoke and poitrels, all of gold,
She fastened. — BRYANT.

τοῦ δ' ἐξ ἀργύρεος ῥυμὸς πέλεν· αὐτὰρ ἐπ' ἄκρῳ
δῆσε χρύσειον καλὸν ζυγὸν, ἐν δὲ λέπαδνα
κάλ' ἔβαλε, χρύσει'·

When Homer wishes to tell us how Agamemnon was dressed, he makes the king put on every article of raiment in our presence: the soft tunic, the great mantle, the beautiful sandals, and the sword. When he is thus fully equipped he grasps his sceptre. We see the clothes while the poet is describing the act of dressing. An inferior writer would have described the clothes down to the minutest fringe, and of the action we should have seen nothing.[1]

μαλακὸν δ' ἔνδυνε χιτῶνα,
καλὸν νηγάτεον, περὶ δὲ μέγα βάλλετο φᾶρος·
ποσσὶ δ' ὑπὸ λιπαροῖσιν ἐδήσατο καλὰ πέδιλα,
ἀμφὶ δ' ἄρ' ὤμοισιν βάλετο ξίφος ἀργυρόηλον.
εἵλετο δὲ σκῆπτρον πατρώϊον, ἄφθιτον αἰεί·

How does he manage when he desires to give a more full and minute picture of the sceptre, which is here called only ancestral and undecaying, as a similar one in another place is only χρυσέοις ἥλοισι πεπάρμενον, — golden-studded? Does he paint for us, besides the golden nails, the wood, and the

[1] Iliad ii. 43–47.

He sat upright and put his tunic on,
Soft, fair, and new, and over that he cast
His ample cloak, and round his shapely feet
Laced the becoming sandals. Next, he hung
Upon his shoulders and his side the sword
With silver studs, and took into his hand
The ancestral sceptre, old but undecayed. — BRYANT.

carved head? He might have done so, had he been writing a description for a book of heraldry, from which at some later day an exact copy was to be made. Yet I have no doubt that many a modern poet would have given such heraldic description in the honest belief that he was really making a picture himself, because he was giving the painter material for one. But what does Homer care how far he outstrips the painter? Instead of a copy, he gives us the history of the sceptre. First we see it in the workshop of Vulcan; then it shines in the hands of Jupiter; now it betokens the dignity of Mercury; now it is the baton of warlike Pelops; and again the shepherd's staff of peace-loving Atreus.[1]

σκῆπτρον, τὸ μὲν Ἥφαιστος κάμε τεύχων·
Ἥφαιστος μὲν δῶκε Διὶ Κρονίωνι ἄνακτι,
αὐτὰρ ἄρα Ζεὺς δῶκε διακτόρῳ Ἀργειφόντῃ·
Ἑρμείας δὲ ἄναξ δῶκεν Πέλοπι πληξίππῳ,
αὐτὰρ ὁ αὖτε Πέλοψ δῶκ' Ἀτρέϊ, ποιμένι λαων·

[1] Iliad ii. 101–108.

He held
The sceptre; Vulcan's skill had fashioned it,
And Vulcan gave it to Saturnian Jove,
And Jove bestowed it on his messenger,
The Argus-queller Hermes. He in turn
Gave it to Pelops, great in horsemanship;
And Pelops passed the gift to Atreus next,
The people's shepherd. Atreus, when he died,
Bequeathed it to Thyestes, rich in flocks;
And last, Thyestes left it to be borne
By Agamemnon, symbol of his rule
O'er many isles and all the Argive realm. —BRYANT.

'Ατρεὺς δὲ θνήσκων ἔλιπεν πολύαρνι Θυέστῃ,
αὐτὰρ ὁ αὖτε Θυέστ' Ἀγαμέμνονι λεῖπε φορῆναι,
πολλῇσιν νήσοισι καὶ Ἄργεϊ παντὶ ἀνάσσειν.

And so at last I know this sceptre better than if a painter should put it before my eyes, or a second Vulcan give it into my hands.

It would not surprise me to find that some one of Homer's old commentators had admired this passage as a perfect allegory of the origin, progress, establishment, and final inheritance of monarchical power among men. I should smile indeed were I to read that the maker of the sceptre, Vulcan, as fire, as that which is of supreme importance to the maintenance of mankind, typified the removal of the necessities which induced the early races of men to subject themselves to a single ruler; that the first king was a son of Time (*Ζεὺς Κρονίων*), revered and venerable, who desired to share his power with a wise and eloquent man, a Mercury (*Διακτόρῳ Ἀργειφόντῃ*), or to resign it wholly to him; that the wise speaker, at the time when the young state was threatened by foreign enemies, delivered his supreme authority to the bravest warrior (*Πέλοπι πληξίππῳ*); that the brave warrior, after having subdued the enemies and secured the safety of the realm, let this power play into the hands of his son, who, as a peace-loving ruler, a beneficent shepherd of his people (*ποιμὴν λαῶν*), introduced comfort and luxury; that thus the way was opened, after his death, for the richest of his relations (*πολύαρν*

Θυέστῃ) to obtain by gifts and bribery, and finally to secure to his family for ever, as a piece of property obtained by purchase, that authority which had originally been conferred as a mark of confidence, and had been regarded by merit rather as a burden than an honor. I should smile at all this, but it would increase my respect for a poet to whom so much could be attributed.

But this is a digression. I am now considering the history of the sceptre as a device for making us linger over a single object, without entering into a tiresome description of its various parts. Again, when Achilles swears by his sceptre to be revenged on Agamemnon for his contemptuous treatment, Homer gives us the history of this sceptre. We see it still green upon the mountains, the axe severs it from the parent trunk, strips it of leaves and bark, and makes it ready to serve the judges of the people, as the token of their godlike office.[1]

> *ναὶ μὰ τόδε σκῆπτρον, τὸ μὲν οὔποτε φύλλα καὶ ὄζους*
> *φύσει, ἐπειδὴ πρῶτα τομὴν ἐν ὄρεσσι λέλοιπεν,*
> *οὐδ᾽ ἀναθηλήσει· περὶ γάρ ῥά ἑ χαλκὸς ἔλεψεν*
> *φύλλα τε καὶ φλοιόν· νῦν αὐτέ μιν υἷες Ἀχαιῶν*
> *ἐν παλάμῃς φορέουσι δικασπόλοι, οἵτε θέμιστας*
> *πρὸς Διὸς εἰρύαται.*

[1] Iliad i. 234–239.

> By this my sceptre, which can never bear
> A leaf or twig, since first it left its stem
> Among the mountains, — for the steel has pared
> Its boughs and bark away, — to sprout no more,
> And now the Achaian judges bear it, — they
> Who guard the laws received from Jupiter.
>
> BRYANT

Homer's object was not so much to describe two staves of different shape and material, as to give us a graphic picture of the different degrees of power which these staves represented. One the work of Vulcan, the other cut upon the hills by an unknown hand; one the old possession of a noble house, the other destined to be grasped by the first comer; one extended by a monarch over many islands and over all Argos, the other borne by one from among the Greeks, who, in connection with others, had been intrusted with the duty of upholding the laws. This was in fact the difference between Agamemnon and Achilles; and Achilles, even in the blindness of his passion, could not but admit it.

Not only when Homer's descriptions have these higher aims in view, but even when his sole object is the picture, he will yet break this up into a sort of history of the object in order that the various parts, which we see side by side in nature, may just as naturally follow each other in his picture, and, as it were, keep pace with the flow of the narrative.

He wants, for instance, to paint us the bow of Pandarus. It is of horn, of a certain length, well polished, and tipped at both ends with gold. What does he do? Does he enumerate these details thus drily one after another? By no means. That would be telling off such a bow, setting it as a copy, but not painting it. He begins with the hunting of the wild goat from whose horns the bow was made. Pandarus had lain in wait for him among the rocks and slain him. Owing to the extraordinary size of the horns, he decided to use them for a bow. They come under the workman's hands, who joins them together, polishes, and tips them. And thus, as I have said, the poet shows us in the process of creation, what the painter can only show us as already existing.[1]

> *τόξον ἐύξοον ἰξάλου αἰγὸς*
> *ἀγρίου, ὅν ῥά ποτ᾽ αὐτὸς στέρνοιο τυχήσας*
> *πέτρης ἐκβαίνοντα, δεδεγμένος ἐν προδοκῇσιν,*
> *βεβλήκει πρὸς στῆθος· ὁ δ᾽ ὕπτιος ἔμπεσε πέτρῃ.*
> *τοῦ κέρα ἐκ κεφαλῆς ἑκκαιδεκάδωρα πεφύκει·*
> *καὶ τὰ μὲν ἀσκήσας κεραοξόος ἤραρε τέκτων,*
> *πᾶν δ᾽ εὖ λειήνας, χρυσέην ἐπέθηκε κορώνην.*

I should never have done, were I to try to write out all the examples of this kind. They will occur in numbers to every one familiar with Homer.

[1] Iliad iv. 105–111.

> He uncovered straight
> His polished bow made of the elastic horns
> Of a wild goat, which, from his lurking-place,
> As once it left its cavern lair, he smote,
> And pierced its breast, and stretched it on the rock.
> Full sixteen palms in length the horns had grown
> From the goat's forehead. These an artisan
> Had smoothed, and, aptly fitting each to each,
> Polished the whole and tipped the work with gold.
>
> BRYANT.

XVII.

But, it may be urged, the signs employed in poetry not only follow each other, but are also arbitrary; and, as arbitrary signs, they are certainly capable of expressing things as they exist in space. Homer himself furnishes examples of this. We have but to call to mind his shield of Achilles to have an instance of how circumstantially and yet poetically a single object can be described according to its coexistent parts.

I will proceed to answer this double objection. I call it double, because a just conclusion must hold, though unsupported by examples, and on the other hand the example of Homer has great weight with me, even when I am unable to justify it by rules.

It is true that since the signs of speech are arbitrary, the parts of a body can by their means be made to follow each other as readily as in nature they exist side by side. But this is a property of the signs of language in general, not of those peculiar to poetry. The prose writer is satisfied with being intelligible, and making his representations plain and clear. But this is not enough for the poet. He desires to present us with images so vivid, that we fancy we have the things themselves before us, and cease for the moment to be conscious of his words, the instruments with which he effects his purpose. That was the point made in the definition given above of a poetical picture. But the poet must always paint; and now let us see in how far bodies, considered in relation to their parts lying together in space, are fit subjects for this painting.

How do we obtain a clear idea of a thing in space? First we observe its separate parts, then the union of these parts, and finally the whole. Our senses perform these various operations with such amazing rapidity as to make them seem but one. This rapidity is absolutely essential to our obtaining an idea of the whole, which is nothing more than the result of the conception of the parts and of their connection with each other. Suppose now that the poet should lead us in proper order from one part of the object to the other; suppose he should succeed in making the connection of these parts perfectly clear to us; how much time will he have consumed?

The details, which the eye takes in at a glance, he enumerates slowly one by one, and it often happens that, by the time he has brought us to the last, we have forgotten the first. Yet from these details we are to form a picture. When we look at an object the various parts are always present to the eye. It can run over them again and again. The ear, however, loses the details it has heard, unless memory retain them. And if they be so retained, what pains and effort it costs to recall their impressions in the proper order and with even the moderate degree of rapidity necessary to the obtaining of a tolerable idea of the whole.

Let us take an example which may be called a masterpiece of its kind.

Dort ragt das hohe Haupt vom edeln Enziane
Weit übern niedern Chor der Pöbelkräuter hin,
Ein ganzes Blumenvolk dient unter seiner Fahne,
Sein blauer Bruder selbst bückt sich und ehret ihn.
Der Blumen helles Gold, in Strahlen umgebogen,
Thürmt sich am Stengel auf, und krönt sein grau Gewand,
Der Blätter glattes Weiss mit tiefem Grün durchzogen,
Strahlt von dem bunten Blitz von feuchtem Diamant.
Gerechtestes Gesetz! dass Kraft sich Zier vermähle,
In einem schönen Leib wohnt eine schön're Seele.

Hier kriecht ein niedrig Kraut, gleich einem grauen Nebel
Dem die Natur sein Blatt im Kreuze hingelegt,
Die holde Blume zeigt die zwei vergöldten Schnäbel,
Die ein von Amethyst gebildter Vogel trägt.
Dort wirft ein glänzend Blatt, in Finger ausgekerbet,
Auf einen hellen Bach den grünen Wiederschein;
Der Blumen zarten Schnee, den matter Purpur färbet,
Schliesst ein gestreifter Stern in weisse Strahlen ein.
Smaragd und Rosen blühn auch auf zertretner Heide,
Und Felsen decken sich mit einem Purpurkleide.[1]

[1] Von Haller's Alps.

The lofty gentian's head in stately grandeur towers
Far o'er the common herd of vulgar weeds and low;
Beneath his banners serve communities of flowers;
His azure brethren, too, in rev'rence to him bow.
The blossom's purest gold in curving radiations
Erect upon the stalk, above its gray robe gleams;
The leaflets' pearly white with deep green variegations
With flashes many-hued of the moist diamond beams.

The learned poet is here painting plants and flowers with great art and in strict accordance with nature, but there is no illusion in his picture. I do not mean that a person who had never seen these plants and flowers could form little or no idea of them from his description. Perhaps all poetical pictures require a previous knowledge of their subject. Neither would I deny that a person possessing such knowledge might derive from the poet a more vivid idea of certain details. I only ask how it is with a conception of the whole. If that is to become more vivid, none of the separate details must stand in undue prominence, but the new illumination must be equally shared by all. Our imagination must be able to embrace them all with equal rapidity in order to form from them in an instant that one harmonious whole which the eye takes in at a glance. Is that the case here? If not, how can it be said, "that the most exact copy produced by a painter is dull and faint compared with this

O Law beneficent! which strength to beauty plighteth,
And to a shape so fair a fairer soul uniteth.

Here on the ground a plant like a gray mist is twining,
In fashion of a cross its leaves by Nature laid;
Part of the beauteous flower, the gilded beak is shining,
Of a fair bird whose shape of amethyst seems made.
There into fingers cleft a polished leaf reposes,
And o'er a limpid brook its green reflection throws;
With rays of white a striped star encloses
The floweret's disk, where pink flushes its tender snows.
Thus on the trodden heath are rose and emerald glowing,
And e'en the rugged rocks are purple banners showing.

poetical description"?[1] It is far inferior to what lines and colors can produce on canvas. The critic who bestowed upon it this exaggerated praise must have regarded it from an entirely false point of view. He must have looked at the foreign graces which the poet has woven into his description, at his idealization of vegetable life, and his development of inward perfections, to which outward beauty serves but as the shell. These he was considering, and not beauty itself or the degree of resemblance and vividness of the image, which painter and poet respectively can give us. Upon this last point every thing depends, and whoever maintains that the lines,

> Der Blumen helles Gold in Strahlen umgebogen,
> Thürmt sich am Stengel auf, und krönt sein grau Gewand,
> Der Blätter glattes Weiss, mit tiefem Grün durchzogen,
> Strahlt von dem bunten Blitz von feuchtem Diamant,

can vie in vividness of impression with a flower-piece by a Huysum, must either never have analyzed his own sensations, or must wilfully ignore them. It might be very pleasant to hear the lines read if we had the flowers in our hand; but, taken by themselves, they say little or nothing. I hear in every word the laborious poet, but the thing itself I am unable to see.

Once more, then, I do not deny that language has the power of describing a corporeal whole according to its parts. It certainly has, because its signs, although consecutive, are nevertheless arbitrary. But I deny that this power exists in language as the

[1] Breitinger's kritische Dichtkunst, vol. ii. p. 807.

instrument of poetry. For illusion, which is the special aim of poetry, is not produced by these verbal descriptions of objects, nor can it ever be so produced. The coexistence of the body comes into collision with the sequence of the words, and although while the former is getting resolved into the latter, the dismemberment of the whole into its parts is a help to us, yet the reunion of these parts into a whole is made extremely difficult, and not infrequently impossible.

Where the writer does not aim at illusion, but is simply addressing the understanding of his readers with the desire of awakening distinct and, as far as possible, complete ideas, then these descriptions of corporeal objects, inadmissible as they are in poetry, are perfectly appropriate. Not only the prose writer, but the didactic poet (for in as far as he is didactic he is no poet) may use them with good effect. Thus Virgil, in his Georgics, describes a cow fit for breeding: —

Optima torvæ
Forma bovis, cui turpe caput, cui plurima cervix,
Et crurum tenus a mento palearia pendent.
Tum longo nullus lateri modus : omnia magna :
Pes etiam, et camuris hirtæ sub cornibus aures.
Nec mihi displiceat maculis insignis et albo,
Aut juga detractans interdumque aspera cornu,
Et faciem tauro propior ; quæque ardua tota,
Et gradiens ima verrit vestigia cauda.[1]

[1] Georg. lib. iii. 51 and 79.
If her large front and neck vast strength denote;
If on her knee the pendulous dewlap float;

Or a handsome colt: —

> Illi ardua cervix,
> Argutumque caput, brevis alvus, obesaque terga,
> Luxuriatque toris animosum pectus, &c.[1]

Here the poet is plainly concerned more with the setting forth of the separate parts than with the effect of the whole. His object is to tell us the characteristics of a handsome colt and a good cow, so that we may judge of their excellence according to the number of these characteristics which they possess. Whether or not all these can be united into a vivid picture was a matter of indifference to him.

Except for this purpose, elaborate pictures of bodily objects, unless helped out by the above-mentioned Homeric device of making an actual series out of their coexistent parts, have always been considered by the best critics as ineffective trifles, requiring little or no genius. "When a poetaster,"

> If curling horns their crescent inward bend,
> And bristly hairs beneath the ear defend;
> If lengthening flanks to bounding measure spread;
> If broad her foot and bold her bull-like head;
> If snowy spots her mottled body stain,
> And her indignant brow the yoke disdain,
> With tail wide-sweeping as she stalks the dews,
> Thus, lofty, large, and long, the mother choose.
>
> DRYDEN.

[1] Georg. lib. iii. 51 and 79.

> Light on his airy crest his slender head,
> His belly short, his loins luxuriant spread;
> Muscle on muscle knots his brawny breast, &c.
>
> DRYDEN.

says Horace, "can do nothing else, he falls to describing a grove, an altar, a brook winding through pleasant meadows, a rushing river, or a rainbow."

> Lucus et ara Dianæ,
> Et properantis aquæ per amœnos ambitus agros,
> Aut flumen Rhenum, aut pluvius describitur arcus.[1]

Pope, when a man, looked back with contempt on the descriptive efforts of his poetic childhood. He expressly enjoined upon every one, who would not prove himself unworthy the name of poet, to abandon as early as possible this fondness for description. A merely descriptive poem he declared to be a feast made up of sauces.[2] Herr Von Kleist, I know, prided himself very little on his "Spring." Had he lived, he would have refashioned it altogether. He wanted to introduce into it some plan, and was meditating how he could best make the crowd of pictures, which seemed to have been drawn at random from the whole vast range of fresh creation, rise in some natural order and follow each other in fitting sequence. He would, at the same time, have done what Marmontel, doubtless with reference to his Eclogues, recommended to several German poets. He would have converted a series of pictures scantily interwoven with mental emotions, into a series of emotions sparingly interspersed with images.[3]

[1] De Art. Poet. 16.
[2] See Appendix, note 37.
[3] See Appendix, note 38.

XVIII.

AND shall Homer nevertheless have fallen into those barren descriptions of material objects?

Let us hope that only a few such passages can be cited. And even those few, I venture to assert, will be found really to confirm the rule, to which they appear to form an exception.

The rule is this, that succession in time is the province of the poet, co-existence in space that of the artist.

To bring together into one and the same picture two points of time necessarily remote, as Mazzuoli does the rape of the Sabine women and the reconciliation effected by them between their husbands and relations; or as Titian does, representing in one piece the whole story of the Prodigal Son, — his dissolute life, his misery, and repentance, — is an encroachment of the painter on the domain of the poet, which good taste can never sanction.

To try to present a complete picture to the reader by enumerating in succession several parts or things which in nature the eye necessarily takes in at a glance, is an encroachment of the poet on the domain of the painter, involving a great effort of the imagination to very little purpose.

Painting and poetry should be like two just and friendly neighbors, neither of whom indeed is allowed to take unseemly liberties in the heart of the other's domain, but who exercise mutual forbearance on the borders, and effect a peaceful settlement for all the petty encroachments which circumstances may compel either to make in haste on the rights of the other.

I will not bring forward in support of this the fact that, in large historical pictures the single moment of time is always somewhat extended, and that perhaps no piece, very rich in figures, can be found, in which every character has exactly the motion and attitude proper to him at that particular moment. The position of some belongs to a preceding point of time, that of others to a later. This is a liberty which the painter must justify by certain subtleties of arrangement, such as placing his figures more in the foreground or background, and thus making them take a more or less immediate interest in what is going on. I will merely quote, in favor of my view, a criticism of Mengs on Raphael's drapery.[1] "There is a reason for all his folds, either in the weight of the material or the tension of the limbs. We can often infer from their present condition what they had been previously. Raphael indeed aimed at giving them significance in this way. We can judge from the folds whether, previously to the present posture, a leg or an arm had been more in front or

[1] Gedanken über die Schönheit und über den Geschmack in der Malerei, p. 69.

more behind, whether a limb had been bent and is now straightening itself, or whether it had been outstretched and is now bending." Here unquestionably the artist unites into one two distinct points of time. For, since the foot in its motion forward is immediately followed by that portion of the garment which rests upon it, — unless indeed the garment be of exceedingly stiff material, in which case it is ill adapted to painting, — there can be no moment at which the drapery assumes in the least degree any other fold than the present posture of the limb demands. If any other be represented, then the fold is that of the preceding moment while the position of the foot is that of the present. Few, however, will be inclined to deal thus strictly with the artist who finds it for his interest to bring these two moments of time before us at once. Who will not rather praise him for having had the wisdom and the courage to commit a slight fault for the sake of greater fulness of expression?

A similar indulgence is due to the poet. The continuity of his imitation permits him, strictly speaking, to touch at one moment on only a single side, a single property of his corporeal objects. But if the happy construction of his language enables him to do this with a single word, why should he not sometimes be allowed to add a second such word? why not a third, if it be worth his while, or even a fourth? As I have said, a ship in Homer is either simply the black ship, or the hollow ship, or the swift ship; at most the well-manned black ship.

That is true of his style in general. Occasionally a passage occurs where he adds a third descriptive epithet:[1] *Καμπύλα κύκλα, χάλκεα, ὀκτάκνημα*, "round, brazen, eight-spoked wheels." Even a fourth: *ἀσπίδα πάντοσε εἴσην, καλὴν, χαλκείην, ἐξήλατον*,[2] "a uniformly smooth, beautiful, brazen, wrought shield." Who will not rather thank than blame him for this little luxuriance, when we perceive its good effect in a few suitable passages?

The true justification of both poet and painter shall not, however, be left to rest upon this analogy of two friendly neighbors. A mere analogy furnishes neither proof nor justification. I justify them in this way. As in the picture the two moments of time follow each other so immediately that we can without effort consider them as one, so in the poem the several touches answering to the different parts and properties in space are so condensed, and succeed each other so rapidly, that we seem to catch them all at once.

Here, as I have said, Homer is greatly aided by his admirable language. It not only allows him all possible freedom in multiplying and combining his epithets, but enables him to arrange them so happily that we are relieved of all awkward suspense with regard to the subject. Some of the modern languages are destitute of one or more of those advantages. Those which, like the French, must have recourse to paraphrase, and convert the *καμπύλα κύκλα, χάλκεα, ὀκτάκνημα* of Homer into "the round

[1] Iliad v. 722. [2] Iliad xii. 296.

wheels which were of brass and had eight spokes," give the meaning, but destroy the picture. The sense is here, however, nothing; the picture every thing. The one without the other turns the most graphic of poets into a tiresome tattler. This fate has often befallen Homer under the pen of the conscientious Madame Dacier. The German language can generally render the Homeric adjectives by equally short equivalents, but it cannot follow the happy arrangement of the Greek. It can say, indeed, "the round, brazen, eight-spoked;" but "wheels" comes dragging after. Three distinct predicates before any subject make but a confused, uncertain picture. The Greek joins the subject with the first predicate and lets the others follow. He says, "round wheels, brazen, eight-spoked." Thus we know at once of what he is speaking, and learn first the thing and then its accidents, which is the natural order of our thoughts. The German language does not possess this advantage. Or shall I say, what really amounts to the same thing, that, although possessing it, the language can seldom use it without ambiguity? For if adjectives be placed after the subject (runde Räder, ehern und achtspeichigt) they are indeclinable, differing in nothing from adverbs, and if referred, as adverbs, to the first verb that is predicated of the subject, the meaning of the whole sentence becomes always distorted, and sometimes entirely falsified.

But I am lingering over trifles and seem to have forgotten the shield of Achilles, that famous picture, which more than all else, caused Homer to be regarded among the ancients as a master of painting.[1] But surely a shield, it may be said, is a single corporeal object, the description of which according to its coexistent parts cannot come within the province of poetry. Yet this shield, its material, its form, and all the figures which occupied its enormous surface, Homer has described, in more than a hundred magnificent lines, so circumstantially and precisely that modern artists have found no difficulty in making a drawing of it exact in every detail.

My answer to this particular objection is, that I have already answered it. Homer does not paint the shield finished, but in the process of creation. Here again he has made use of the happy device of substituting progression for coexistence, and thus converted the tiresome description of an object into a graphic picture of an action. We see not the shield, but the divine master-workman employed upon it. Hammer and tongs in hand he approaches the anvil; and, after having forged the plates from the rough metal, he makes the pictures designed for its decoration rise from the brass, one by one, under his finer blows. Not till the whole is finished do we lose sight of him. At last it is done; and we wonder at the work, but with the believing wonder of an eye-witness who has seen it a-making.

The same cannot be said of the shield of Æneas in Virgil. The Roman poet either failed to see the fineness of his model, or the things which he wished

[1] Dionysius Halicarnass. in Vita Homeri apud Th. Gale in Opusc. Mythol. p. 401.

to represent upon his shield seemed to him not of such a kind as to allow of their being executed before our eyes. They were prophecies, which the god certainly could not with propriety have uttered in our presence as distinctly as the poet explains them in his work. Prophecies, as such, require a darker speech, in which the names of those persons to come, whose fortunes are predicted, cannot well be spoken. In these actual names, however, lay, it would seem, the chief point of interest to the poet and courtier.[1] But this, though it excuse him, does not do away with the disagreeable effect of his departure from the Homeric method, as all readers of taste will admit. The preparations made by Vulcan are nearly the same in Homer as in Virgil. But while in Homer we see, besides the preparations for the work, the work itself, Virgil, after showing us the god at work with his Cyclops,

> Ingentem clypeum informant . . .
> . . . Alii ventosis follibus auras
> Accipiunt, redduntque; alii stridentia tingunt
> Æra lacu. Gemit impositis incudibus antrum.
> Illi inter sese multa vi brachia tollunt
> In numerum, versantque tenaci forcipe massam,[2]

[1] See Appendix, note 39.

[2] Æneid lib. viii. 447.

> Their artful hands a shield prepare.
> One stirs the fire, and one the bellows blows;
> The hissing steel is in the smithy drowned;
> The grot with beaten anvils groans around.
> By turns their arms advance in equal time,
> By turns their hands descend and hammers chime;
> They turn the glowing mass with crooked tongs.
> DRYDEN.

suddenly drops the curtain and transports us to a wholly different scene. We are gradually led into the valley where Venus appears, bringing Æneas the arms that in the mean while have been finished. She places them against the trunk of an oak; and, after the hero has sufficiently stared at them, and wondered over them, and handled them, and tried them, the description or picture of the shield begins, which grows so cold and tedious from the constantly recurring "here is," and "there is," and "near by stands," and "not far from there is seen," that all Virgil's poetic grace is needed to prevent it from becoming intolerable. Since, moreover, this description is not given by Æneas, who delights in the mere figures without any knowledge of their import,

. . . rerumque ignarus imagine gaudet,

nor by Venus, although she might be supposed to know as much about the fortunes of her dear grandson as her good-natured husband, but by the poet himself, the action meanwhile necessarily remains at a stand-still. Not a single one of the characters takes part; nor is what follows in the least affected by the representations on the shield. The subtle courtier, helping out his material with every manner of flattering allusion, is apparent throughout; but no trace do we see of the great genius, who trusts to the intrinsic merit of his work, and despises all extraneous means of awakening interest. The shield of Æneas is therefore, in fact, an interpolation, intended solely to flatter the pride of the Romans; a foreign brook with which the poet seeks to give fresh movement to his stream. The shield of Achilles, on the contrary, is the outgrowth of its own fruitful soil. For a shield was needed; and, since even what is necessary never comes from the hands of deity devoid of beauty, the shield had to be ornamented. The art was in treating these ornamentations as such, and nothing more; in so weaving them into the material that when we look at that we cannot but see them. This could be accomplished only by the method which Homer adopted. Homer makes Vulcan devise decorations, because he is to make a shield worthy of a divine workman. Virgil seems to make him fashion the shield for the sake of the decorations, since he deems these of sufficient importance to deserve a special description long after the shield is finished.

XIX.

THE objections brought against Homer's shield by the elder Scaliger, Perrault, Terrasson, and others, are well known, as are also the answers of Madame Dacier, Boivin, and Pope. But these latter, it seems to me, have gone somewhat too far, and confiding in the justness of their cause have asserted things incorrect in themselves and contributing little to the poet's justification.

In answer to the chief objection, that Homer had burdened his shield with more figures than there could possibly have been room for, Boivin undertook to show in a drawing how the necessary space might be obtained. His idea of the various concentric circles was very ingenious, although there is no foundation for it in the poet's words and nothing anywhere to indicate that shields divided in this way were known to the ancients. Since Homer calls it (*σάκος πάντοσε δεδαιδαλωμένον*) a shield, artistically wrought on all sides, I should prefer to gain the required space by turning to account the concave surface. A proof that the old artists did not leave this empty is furnished in the shield of Minerva by Phidias.[1] But not only does Boivin fail to seize

[1] See Appendix, note 40.

this advantage, but, by separating into two or three pictures what the poet evidently meant for one, he unnecessarily multiplies the representations while diminishing the space by one-half. I know the motive which led him to this, but it was one by which he should not have allowed himself to be influenced. He should have shown his opponents the unreasonableness of their demands, instead of trying to satisfy them.

An example will make my meaning clear. When Homer says of one of the two cities:[1]

> λαοὶ δ' εἰν ἀγορῇ ἔσαν ἀθρόοι· ἔνθα δὲ νεῖκος
> ὠρώρει δύο δ' ἄνδρες ἐνείκεον εἵνεκα ποινῆς
> ἀνδρὸς ἀποφθιμένου· ὁ μὲν εὔχετο πάντ' ἀποδοῦναι,
> δήμῳ πιφαύσκων, ὁ δ' ἀναίνετο μηδὲν ἑλέσθαι·
> ἄμφω δ' ἱέσθην ἐπὶ ἴστορι πεῖραρ ἑλέσθαι.

[1] Iliad xviii. 497–508.

> Meanwhile a multitude
> Was in the forum where a strife went on, —
> Two men contending for a fine, the price
> Of one who had been slain. Before the crowd
> One claimed that he had paid the fine, and one
> Denied that aught had been received, and both
> Called for the sentence which should end the strife.
> The people clamored for both sides, for both
> Had eager friends; the herald held the crowd
> In check; the elders, upon polished stones,
> Sat in a sacred circle. Each one took
> In turn a herald's sceptre in his hand,
> And rising gave his sentence. In the midst
> Two talents lay in gold, to be the meed
> Of him whose juster judgment should prevail.
>
> BRYANT.

λαοὶ δ' ἀμφοτέροισιν ἐπήπυον, ἀμφὶς ἀρωγοί.
κήρυκες δ' ἄρα λαὸν ἐρήτυον· οἱ δὲ γέροντες
εἵατ' ἐπὶ ξεστοῖσι λίθοις ἱερῷ ἐνὶ κύκλῳ,
σκῆπτρα δὲ κηρύκων ἐν χέρσ' ἔχον ηεροφώνων·
τοῖσιν ἔπειτ' ἤϊσσον, ἀμοιβηδὶς δὲ δίκαζον.
κεῖτο δ' ἄρ' ἐν μέσσοισι δύω χρυσοῖο τάλαντα,

he refers, as I understand him, to but a single picture, that of a public lawsuit about the contested payment of a considerable fine for the committal of a murder. The artist, who is to execute this design, can use but a single moment of the action, — that of the accusation, of the examination of witnesses, of the pronouncing of the sentence, or any other preceding or following or intervening moment which may seem to him most fitting. This single moment he makes as pregnant as possible, and reproduces it with all that power of illusion which in the presentation of visible objects art possesses above poetry. Left far behind in this respect, what remains to the poet, if his words are to paint the same design with any degree of success, but to avail himself of his peculiar advantages? These are the liberty of extending his representation over what preceded, as well as what was to follow, the artist's single point of time, and the power of showing not only what the artist shows, but what he has to leave to our imagination. Only by using these advantages can the poet raise himself to a level with the artist. Their works most resemble each other when their effect is equally vivid; not when one brings before the imagination through the ear neither more nor less than the other presents to the eye. Had Boivin defended the passage in Homer according to this principle, he would not have divided it into as many separate pictures as he thought he detected distinct points of time. All that Homer relates could not, indeed, be united in a single picture. The accusation and the denial, the summoning of the witnesses and the shouts of the divided populace, the efforts of the heralds to quiet the tumult and the sentence of the judges, are things successive in time, not coexistent in space. But what is not actually in the picture is there virtually, and the only true way of representing an actual picture in words is to combine what virtually exists in it with what is absolutely visible. The poet who allows himself to be bound by the limits of art may furnish data for a picture, but can never create one of his own.

The picture of the beleagured city[1] Boivin divides likewise into three. He might as well have made twelve out of it as three. For since he has once for all failed to grasp the spirit of the poet, and requires him to be bound by the unities of a material picture, he might have discovered many more violations of these unities. In fact he ought almost to have devoted a separate space on the shield to every separate touch of the poet. In my opinion Homer has but ten different pictures on the whole shield, every one of which he introduces with ἐν μὲν ἔτευξε, or ἐν δὲ ποίησε, or ἐν δ' ἐτίθει, or ἐν δὲ ποίκιλλε Ἀμφιγυήεις, "on it he wrought," "on it he placed,"

[1] Iliad xviii. 509–540.

"on it he formed," "on it Vulcan skilfully fashioned."[1] In the absence of these introductory words we have no right to suppose a distinct picture. On the contrary every thing which they cover must be regarded as a single whole, wanting in nothing but the arbitrary concentration into one moment of time, which the poet was in no way bound to observe. Had he observed this, and, by strictly limiting himself to it, excluded every little feature which in the material representation would have been inconsistent with this unity of time; had he in fact done what his cavillers require, — these gentlemen would indeed have had no fault to find with him, but neither would any person of taste have found aught to admire.

Pope not only accepted Boivin's drawing, but thought he was doing a special service by showing that every one of these mutilated pieces was in accordance with the strictest rules of painting, as laid down at the present day. Contrast, perspective, the three unities, he found, were all observed in the best possible manner. And although well aware that, according to the testimony of good and trustworthy witnesses, painting at the time of the Trojan war was still in its cradle, he supposes either that Homer, instead of being bound by the achievements of painting at that time or in his own day, must in virtue of his godlike genius have anticipated all that art should in future be able to accomplish, or else that the witnesses could not have been so entirely worthy of faith that the direct testimony of this

[1] See Appendix, note 41.

artistic shield should not be preferred to theirs. Whoever will, may accept the former supposition: the latter, surely, no one will be persuaded to adopt who knows any thing more of the history of art than the date of the historians. That painting in the time of Homer was still in its infancy he believes, not merely on the authority of Pliny, or some other writer, but chiefly because, judging from the works of art mentioned by the ancients, he sees that even centuries later no great progress had been made. The pictures of Polygnotus, for instance, by no means stand the test which Pope thinks can be successfully applied to Homer's shield. The two great works by this master at Delphi, of which Pausanias has left a circumstantial description,[1] were evidently wholly wanting in perspective. The ancients had no knowledge of this branch of art, and what Pope adduces as proof that Homer understood it, only proves that he has a very imperfect understanding of it himself.[2]

"That Homer," he says, "was not a stranger to aerial perspective appears in his expressly marking the distance of object from object. He tells us, for instance, that the two spies lay a little remote from the other figures, and that the oak under which was spread the banquet of the reapers stood apart. What he says of the valley sprinkled all over with cottages and flocks appears to be a description of a large country in perspective. And, indeed, a general argument for this may be drawn from the number of figures on the shield, which could not be all expressed

[1] Phocic. cap. xxv.-xxxi. [2] See Appendix, note 42.

in their full size; and this is therefore a sort of proof that the art of lessening them according to perspective was known at that time." The mere representing of an object at a distance as smaller than it would be if nearer the eye, by no means constitutes perspective in a picture. Perspective requires a single point of view; a definite, natural horizon; and this was wanting in the old pictures. In the paintings of Polygnotus the ground, instead of being level, rose so decidedly at the back that the figures which were meant to stand behind seemed to be standing above one another. If this was the usual position of the various figures and groups, — and that it was so may fairly be concluded from the old bas-reliefs, where those behind always stand higher than those in front, and look over their heads, — then we may reasonably take it for granted in Homer, and should not unnecessarily dismember those representations of his, which according to this treatment might be united in a single picture. The double scene in the peaceful city, through whose streets a joyous marriage train was moving at the same time that an important trial was going on in the market-place, requires thus no double picture. Homer could very well think of it as one, since he imagined himself to be overlooking the city from such a height as to command at once a view of the streets and the market.

My opinion is that perspective in pictures came incidentally from scene-painting, which was already in its perfection. But the applications of its rules to a single smooth surface was evidently no easy matter; for, even in the later paintings found among the antiquities of Herculaneum, there are many and various offences against perspective, which would now hardly be excusable even in a beginner.[1]

But I will spare myself the labor of collecting my desultory observations on a point whereon I may hope to receive complete satisfaction from Winkelmann's promised "History of Art."[2]

[1] Betrachtungen über die Malerei, p. 185.
[2] Written in 1763.

XX.

To return, then, to my road, if a saunterer can be said to have a road.

What I have been saying of bodily objects in general applies with even more force to those which are beautiful.

Physical beauty results from the harmonious action of various parts which can be taken in at a glance. It therefore requires that these parts should lie near together; and, since things whose parts lie near together are the proper subjects of painting, this art and this alone can imitate physical beauty.

The poet, who must necessarily detail in succession the elements of beauty, should therefore desist entirely from the description of physical beauty as such. He must feel that these elements arranged in a series cannot possibly produce the same effect as in juxtaposition; that the concentrating glance which we try to cast back over them immediately after their enumeration, gives us no harmonious picture; and that to conceive the effect of certain eyes, a certain mouth and nose taken together, unless we can recall a similar combination of such parts in nature or art, surpasses the power of human imagination.

Here again Homer is the model of all models. He says, Nireus was fair; Achilles was fairer; Helen was of godlike beauty. But he is nowhere betrayed into a more detailed description of these beauties. Yet the whole poem is based upon the loveliness of Helen. How a modern poet would have revelled in descriptions of it!

Even Constantinus Manasses sought to adorn his bald chronicle with a picture of Helen. I must thank him for the attempt, for I really should not know where else to turn for so striking an example of the folly of venturing on what Homer's wisdom forbore to undertake. When I read in him:[1]

ην ἡ γυνὴ περικαλλὴς, εὔοφρυς, εὐχρουστάτη,
εὐπάρειος, εὐπρόσωπος, βοῶπις, χιονόχρους,
ἑλικοβλέφαρος, ἁβρὰ, χαρίτων γέμον ἄλσος,
λευκοβραχίων, τρυφερὰ, κάλλος ἀντικρὺς ἔμπνουν,
τὸ πρόσωπον καταλευκὸν, ἡ παρειὰ ῥοδόχρους,
τὸ πρόσωπον ἐπίχαρι, τὸ βλέφαρον ὡραῖον,
κάλλος ἀνεπιτήδευτον, ἀβάπτιστον, αὐτόχρουν,
ἔβαπτε τὴν λευκότητα ῥοδοχρία πυρινή.

1 "She was a woman right beautiful, with fine eyebrows, of clearest complexion, beautiful cheeks; comely, with large, full eyes, with snow-white skin, quick-glancing, graceful; a grove filled with graces, fair-armed, voluptuous, breathing beauty undisguised. The complexion fair, the cheek rosy, the countenance pleasing, the eye blooming; a beauty unartificial, untinted, of its natural color, adding brightness to the brightest cherry, as if one should dye ivory with resplendent purple. Her neck long, of dazzling whiteness; whence she was called the swan-born, beautiful Helen."

ὡς εἴ τις τὸν ἐλέφαντα βάψει λαμπρᾷ πορφύρᾳ.
δειρὴ μακρὰ, καταλευκὸς, ὅθεν ἐμυθουργήθη
κυκνογενῆ τὴν εὔοπτον Ἑλένην χρηματίζειν,

it is like seeing stones rolled up a mountain,[1] on whose summit they are to be built into a gorgeous edifice; but which all roll down of themselves on the other side. What picture does this crowd of words leave behind? How did Helen look? No two readers out of a thousand would receive the same impression of her.

But political verses by a monk are, it is true, no poetry. Let us hear Ariosto describe his enchantress Alcina:[2]—

[1] See Appendix, note 43.

[2] Orlando Furioso, canto vii. st. 11–15.

Her shape is of such perfect symmetry,
As best to feign the industrious painter knows;
With long and knotted tresses; to the eye
Not yellow gold with brighter lustre glows.
Upon her tender cheek the mingled dye
Is scattered of the lily and the rose.
Like ivory smooth, the forehead gay and round
Fills up the space and forms a fitting bound.

Two black and slender arches rise above
Two clear black eyes, say suns of radiant light,
Which ever softly beam and slowly move;
Round these appears to sport in frolic flight,
Hence scattering all his shafts, the little Love,
And seems to plunder hearts in open sight.
Thence, through 'mid visage, does the nose descend,
Where envy finds not blemish to amend.

As if between two vales, which softly curl,
The mouth with vermeil tint is seen to glow;

Di persona era tanto ben formata,
Quanto mai finger san pittori industri.
Con bionda chioma, lunga e annodata,
Oro non è, che piu risplenda e lustri.
Spargeasi per la guancia delicata
Misto color di rose e di ligustri.
Di terso avorio era la fronte lieta,
Che lo spazio finia con giusta meta.

Sotto due negri, e sottilissimi archi
Son due negri, occhi, anzi due chiari soli
Pietosi a riguardar, a mover parchi,
Intorno a cui par ch' Amor scherzi, e voli,

Within are strung two rows of orient pearl,
Which her delicious lips shut up or show,
Of force to melt the heart of any churl,
However rude, hence courteous accents flow;
And here that gentle smile receives its birth,
Which opes at will a paradise on earth.

Like milk the bosom, and the neck of snow;
Round is the neck, and full and round the breast;
Where, fresh and firm, two ivory apples grow,
Which rise and fall, as, to the margin pressed
By pleasant breeze, the billows come and go.
Not prying Argus could discern the rest.
Yet might the observing eye of things concealed
Conjecture safely from the charms revealed.

To all her arms a just proportion bear,
And a white hand is oftentimes descried,
Which narrow is and somedeal long, and where
No knot appears nor vein is signified.
For finish of that stately shape and rare,
A foot, neat, short, and round beneath is spied.
Angelic visions, creatures of the sky,
Concealed beneath no covering veil can lie.

WILLIAM STEWART ROSE.

E ch' indi tutta la faretra scarchi,
E che visibilmente i cori involi.
Quindi il naso per mezzo il viso scende
Che non trova l' invidia ove l' emende.

Sotto quel sta, quasi fra due vallette,
La bocca sparsa di natio cinabro,
Quivi due filze son di perle elette,
Che chiude, ed apre un bello e dolce labro;
Quindi escon le cortesi parolette,
Da render molle ogni cor rozzo e scabro;
Quivi si forma quel soave riso,
Ch' apre a sua posta in terra il paradiso.

Bianca neve è il pel collo, e 'l petto latte,
Il collo è tondo, il petto colmo e largo;
Due pome acerbe, e pur d' avorio fatte,
Vengono e van, come onda al primo margo,
Quando piacevole aura il mar combatte.
Non potria l' altre parti veder Argo,
Ben si può giudicar, che corrisponde,
A quel ch' appar di fuor, quel che s' asconde.

Mostran le braccia sua misura giusta,
Et la candida man spesso si vede,
Lunghetta alquanto, e di larghezza angusta,
Dove nè nodo appar, nè vena eccede.
Si vede al fin de la persona augusta
Il breve, asciutto, e ritondetto piede.
Gli angelici sembianti nati in cielo
Non si ponno celar sotto alcun velo.

Milton, speaking of Pandemonium, says: —

The work some praise, and some the architect.

Praise of one, then, is not always praise of the other. A work of art may merit great approbation without redounding much to the credit of the artist; and again, an artist may justly claim our admiration, even when his work does not entirely satisfy us. By bearing this in mind we can often reconcile contradictory judgments, as in the present case. Dolce, in his dialogues on painting, makes Aretino speak in terms of the highest praise of the above-quoted stanzas,[1] while I select them as an instance of painting without picture. We are both right. Dolce admires the knowledge of physical beauty which the poet shows: I consider only the effect which this knowledge, conveyed in words, produces on my imagination. Dolce concludes from this knowledge that good poets are no less good painters: I, judging from the effect, conclude that what painters can best express by lines and colors is least capable of expression in words. Dolce recommends Ariosto's description to all painters as a perfect model of a beautiful woman: I recommend it to all poets as the most instructive of warnings not to attempt, with still greater want of success, what could not but fail when tried by an Ariosto.

It may be that when the poet says, —

> Di persona era tanto ben formata,
> Quanto mai finger san pittori industri,

he proves himself to have had a complete knowledge of the laws of perspective, such as only the most industrious artist can acquire from a study of nature and of ancient art.[2]

In the words, —

[1] See Appendix, note 44. [2] See Appendix, note 45.

> Spargeasi per la guancia delicata
> Misto color di rose e di ligustri,

he may show himself to be a perfect master of color, — a very Titian.[1] His comparing Alcina's hair to gold, instead of calling it golden hair, may be taken as proof that he objected to the use of actual gold in coloring.[2] We may even discover in the descending nose the profile of those old Greek noses, afterwards borrowed by Roman artists from the Greek masterpieces.[3] Of what use is all this insight and learning to us readers who want to fancy we are looking at a beautiful woman, and desire to feel that gentle quickening of the pulses which accompanies the sight of actual beauty? The poet may know the relations from which beauty springs, but does that make us know them? Or, if we know them, does he show them to us here? or does he help us in the least to call up a vivid image of them?

> A brow that forms a fitting bound,
> Che lo spazio finia con giusta meta;
> A nose where envy itself finds nothing to amend,
> Che non trova l' invidia, ove l' emende;
> A hand, narrow, and somewhat long,
> Lunghetta alquanto, e di larghezza angusta;

what sort of a picture do these general formulæ give us? In the mouth of a drawing-master, directing his pupils' attention to the beauties of the academic model, they might have some meaning. For the

[1] See Appendix, note 46. [2] See Appendix, note 47.
[3] See Appendix, note 48.

students would have but to look at the model to see the fitting bounds of the gay forehead, the fine cut of the nose, and the slenderness of the pretty hand. But in the poem I see nothing, and am only tormented by the futility of all my attempts to see any thing.

In this respect Virgil, by imitating Homer's reticence, has achieved tolerable success. His Dido is only the most beautiful (*pulcherrima*) Dido. Any further details which he may give, have reference to her rich ornaments and magnificent dress.

> Tandem progreditur . . .
> Sidoniam picto chlamydem circumdata limbo:
> Cui pharetra ex auro, crines nodantur in aurum,
> Aurea purpuream subnectit fibula vestem.[1]

If, on this account, any should apply to him what the old artist said to one of his pupils who had painted a gayly decked Helen, — "Since you could not paint her beautiful, you have painted her rich," — Virgil would answer: "I am not to blame that I could not paint her beautiful. The fault lies in the limits of my art, within which it is my merit to have kept."

I must not forget here the two odes of Anacreon wherein he analyzes the beauty of his mistress and

[1] Æneid iv. 136.

> The queen at length appears;
> A flowered cymar with golden fringe she wore,
> And at her back a golden quiver bore;
> Her flowing hair a golden caul restrains;
> A golden clasp the Tyrian robe sustains. — DRYDEN.

of Bathyllus.[1] The device which he uses entirely justifies the analysis. He imagines that he has before him a painter who is working from his description. "Thus paint me the hair," he says; "thus the brow, the eyes, the mouth; thus the neck and bosom, the thighs and hands." As the artist could execute but one detail at a time, the poet was obliged to give them to him thus piecemeal. His object is not to make us see and feel, in these spoken directions to the painter, the whole beauty of the beloved object. He is conscious of the inadequacy of all verbal expression; and for that reason summons to his aid the expression of art, whose power of illusion he so extols, that the whole song seems rather a eulogium of art than of his lady. He sees not the picture but herself, and fancies she is about to open her mouth to speak.

ἀπέχει· βλέπω γὰρ ἀυτήν.
τάχα, κηρέ, καὶ λαλήσεις.

So, too, in his ode to Bathyllus, the praises of the beautiful boy are so mingled with praises of art and the artist, that we are in doubt in whose honor the song was really written. He selects the most beautiful parts from various pictures, the parts for which the pictures were remarkable. He takes the neck from an Adonis, breast and hands from a Mercury, the thighs from a Pollux, the belly from a Bacchus, until he has the whole Bathyllus as a finished Apollo from the artist's hand.

[1] Od. xxviii., xxix.

μετὰ δὲ πρόσωπον ἔστω,
τὸν Ἀδώνιδος παρελθὼν,
ἐλεφάντινος τράχηλος·
μεταμάζιον δὲ ποίει
διδύμας τε χεῖρας Ἑρμου,
Πολυδεύκεος δὲ μηρούς,
Διονυσίην δὲ νηδύν.

. . . .

τὸν Ἀπόλλωνα δὲ τοῦτον
καθελών, ποίει Βάθυλλον.

Thus Lucian, to give an idea of the beauty of Panthea, points to the most beautiful female statues by the old sculptors.[1] What is this but a confession that here language of itself is powerless; that poetry stammers, and eloquence grows dumb, unless art serve as interpreter.

[1] Εἰκόνες, § 3, T. ii. p. 461 (edit. Reitz).

XXI.

But are we not robbing poetry of too much by taking from her all pictures of physical beauty?

Who seeks to take them from her? We are only warning her against trying to arrive at them by a particular road, where she will blindly grope her way in the footsteps of a sister art without ever reaching the goal. We are not closing against her other roads whereon art can follow only with her eyes.

Homer himself, who so persistently refrains from all detailed descriptions of physical beauty, that we barely learn, from a passing mention, that Helen had white arms [1] and beautiful hair,[2] even he manages nevertheless to give us an idea of her beauty, which far surpasses any thing that art could do. Recall the passage where Helen enters the assembly of the Trojan elders. The venerable men see her coming, and one says to the others: [3] —

[1] Iliad iii. 121. [2] Ibid. 319.

[3] Ibid. 156–158.

> Small blame is theirs if both the Trojan knights
> And brazen-mailed Achaians have endured
> So long so many evils for the sake
> Of that one woman. She is wholly like
> In feature to the deathless goddesses. — Bryant.

Οὐ νέμεσις Τρῶας καὶ ἐϋκνήμιδας Ἀχαιοὺς
τοιῇδ' ἀμφὶ γυναικὶ πολὺν χρόνον ἄλγεα πάσχειν·
αἰνῶς ἀθανάτῃσι θεῇς εἰς ὦπα ἔοικεν.

What can give a more vivid idea of her beauty than that cold-blooded age should deem it well worth the war which had cost so much blood and so many tears?

What Homer could not describe in its details, he shows us by its effect. Paint us, ye poets, the delight, the attraction, the love, the enchantment of beauty, and you have painted beauty itself. Who can think of Sappho's beloved, the sight of whom, as she confesses, robs her of sense and thought, as ugly? We seem to be gazing on a beautiful and perfect form, when we sympathize with the emotions which only such a form can produce. It is not Ovid's minute description of the beauties of his Lesbia, —

> Quos humeros, quales vidi tetigique lacertos!
> Forma papillarum quam fuit apta premi!
> Quam castigato planus sub pectore venter!
> Quantum et quale latus! quam juvenile femur!

that makes us fancy we are enjoying the same sight which he enjoyed; but because he gives the details with a sensuousness which stirs the passions.

Yet another way in which poetry surpasses art in the description of physical beauty, is by turning beauty into charm. Charm is beauty in motion, and therefore less adapted to the painter than the poet. The painter can suggest motion, but his figures are really destitute of it. Charm therefore in a picture becomes grimace, while in poetry it remains what it is, a transitory beauty, which we would fain see repeated. It comes and goes, and since we can recall a motion more vividly and easily than mere forms and colors, charm must affect us more strongly than beauty under the same conditions. All that touches and pleases in the picture of Alcina is charm. Her eyes impress us not from their blackness and fire, but because they are —

> Pietosi a riguardar, a mover parchi,

they move slowly and with gracious glances, because Cupid sports around them and shoots from them his arrows. Her mouth pleases, not because vermilion lips enclose two rows of orient pearls, but because of the gentle smile, which opens a paradise on earth, and of the courteous accents that melt the rudest heart. The enchantment of her bosom lies not so much in the milk and ivory and apples, that typify its whiteness and graceful form, as in its gentle heavings, like the rise and fall of waves under a pleasant breeze.

> Due pome acerbe, e pur d' avorio fatte,
> Vengono e van, come onda al primo margo,
> Quando piacevole aura il mar combatte.

I am convinced that such traits as these, compressed into one or two stanzas, would be far more effective than the five over which Ariosto has spread them, interspersed with cold descriptions of form much too learned for our sensibilities.

Anacreon preferred the apparent absurdity of requiring impossibilities of the artist, to leaving the image of his mistress unenlivened with these mobile charms.

τρυφεροῦ δ' ἔσω γενείου
περὶ λυγδίνῳ τραχήλῳ
Χάριτες πέτοιντο πᾶσαι.

He bids the artist let all the graces hover about her tender chin and marble neck. How so? literally? But that is beyond the power of art. The painter could give the chin the most graceful curve and the prettiest dimple, *Amoris digitulo impressum* (for the ἔσω here seems to me to mean dimple); he could give the neck the softest pink, but that is all. The motion of that beautiful neck, the play of the muscles, now deepening and now half concealing the dimple, the essential charm exceeded his powers. The poet went to the limits of his art in the attempt to give us a vivid picture of beauty, in order that the painter might seek the highest expression in his. Here we have, therefore, a fresh illustration of what was urged above, that the poet, even when speaking of a painting or statue, is not bound to confine his description within the limits of art.

XXII.

ZEUXIS painted a Helen, and had the courage to write beneath his picture those famous lines of Homer wherein the elders express their admiration of her beauty. Never did painting and poetry engage in closer rivalry. Victory remained undecided, and both deserved to be crowned.

For as the wise poet showed us only in its effects the beauty which he felt the impossibility of describing in detail, so the equally wise painter exhibited beauty solely through its details, deeming it unworthy of his art to have recourse to any outward aids. His whole picture was the naked figure of Helen. For it was probably the same that he painted for the people of Cortona.[1]

Let us, for curiosity's sake, compare with this Caylus's picture as sketched for modern artists from the same lines of Homer.

"Helen, covered with a white veil, appears in the midst of several old men, Priam among the number, who should be at once recognizable by the emblems of his royal dignity. The artist must especially exert his skill to make us feel the triumph of beauty

[1] Val. Maximus lib. iii. cap. 7. Dionysius Halicarnass. Art. Rhet. cap. 12. περὶ λογῶν ἐξετάσεως.

in the eager glances and expressions of astonished admiration on the countenances of the old men. The scene is over one of the gates of the town. The background of the painting may be lost either in the open sky or against the higher buildings of the town. The first would be the bolder, but the one would be as suitable as the other."

Imagine this picture, executed by the greatest master of our time, and compare it with the work of Zeuxis. Which will show the real triumph of beauty? This, where I feel it myself, or that, where I am to infer it from the grimaces of admiring graybeards? "Turpe senilis amor!" Looks of desire make the most reverend face ridiculous, and an old man who shows the cravings of youth is an object of disgust. This reproach cannot be brought against the Homeric elders. Theirs is but a passing spark of feeling which wisdom instantly stifles; an emotion which does honor to Helen without disgracing themselves. They acknowledge their admiration, but add at once,[1] —

> *ἀλλὰ καὶ ὣς, τοίη περ ἐοῦσ', ἐν νηυσὶ νεέσθω,*
> *μηδ' ἡμῖν τεκέεσσί τ' ὀπίσσω πῆμα λίποιτο.*

This decision saves them from being the old coxcombs which they look like in Caylus's picture. And what is the sight that fixes their eager looks? A veiled, muffled figure. Is that Helen? I cannot

[1] So be it; let her, peerless as she is,
Return on board the fleet, nor stay to bring
Disaster upon us and all our race. — BRYANT.

conceive what induced Caylus to make her wear a veil. Homer, to be sure, expressly gives her one,

> *αὐτίκα δ' ἀργεννῇσι καλυψαμένη ὀθόνῃσιν*
> *ὡρμᾶτ' ἐκ θαλάμοιο,*

"She left her chamber, robed and veiled in white,"

but only to cross the street in. And although he makes the elders express their admiration before she could have had time to take it off or throw it back, yet they were not seeing her then for the first time. Their confession need not therefore have been caused by the present hasty glance. They might often have felt what, on this occasion, they first acknowledged. There is nothing of this in the picture. When I behold the ecstasy of those old men, I want to see the cause, and, as I say, am exceedingly surprised to perceive nothing but a veiled, muffled figure, at which they are staring with such devotion. What of Helen is there? Her white veil and something of her outline, as far as outline can be traced beneath drapery. But perhaps the Count did not mean that her face should be covered. In that case, although his words — "Hélène couverte d'un voile blanc" — hardly admit of such an interpretation, another point excites my surprise. He recommends to the artist great care in the expression of the old men's faces, and wastes not a word upon the beauty of Helen's. This modest beauty, approaching timidly, her eyes moist with repentant tears, — is, then, the highest beauty so much a matter of course to our artists, that they need not be reminded of it? or is expression more than beauty? or is it with pictures as with the stage, where we are accustomed to accept the ugliest of actresses for a ravishing princess, if her prince only express the proper degree of passion for her.

Truly this picture of Caylus would be to that of Zeuxis as pantomime to the most sublime of poetry.

Homer was unquestionably more read formerly than now, yet we do not find mention of many pictures drawn from him even by the old artists.[1] They seem diligently to have availed themselves of any individual physical beauties which he may have pointed out. They painted these, well knowing that in this department alone they could vie with the poet with any chance of success. Zeuxis painted besides Helen a Penelope, and the Diana of Apelles was the goddess of Homer attended by her nymphs.

I will take this opportunity of saying that the passage in Pliny referring to this picture of Apelles needs correcting.[2] But to paint scenes from Homer merely because they afforded a rich composition, striking contrasts, and artistic shading, seems not to have been to the taste of the old artists; nor could it be, so long as art kept within the narrow limits of its own high calling. They fed upon the spirit of the poet, and filled their imagination with his noblest traits. The fire of his enthusiasm kindled theirs. They saw and felt with him. Thus their works became copies of the Homeric, not in the relation of

1 Fabricii Biblioth. Græc. lib. ii. cap. 6, p. 345.

2 See Appendix, note 49.

portrait to original, but in the relation of a son to a father, — like, but different. The whole resemblance often lies in a single trait, the other parts being alike in nothing but in their harmony with that.

Since, moreover, the Homeric masterpieces of poetry were older than any masterpiece of art, for Homer had observed nature with the eye of an artist before either Phidias or Apelles, the artists naturally found ready made in his poems many valuable observations, which they had not yet had time to make for themselves. These they eagerly seized upon, in order that, through Homer, they might copy nature. Phidias acknowledged that the lines,[1] —

Ἦ καὶ κυανέῃσιν ἐπ' ὀφρύσι νεῦσε Κρονίων·
ἀμβρόσιαι δ' ἄρα χαῖται ἐπεῤῥώσαντο ἄνακτος
κρατὸς ἀπ' ἀθανάτοιο· μέγαν δ' ἐλέλιξεν Ὄλυμπον,

served him as the model of his Olympian Jupiter, and that only through their help had he succeeded in making a godlike countenance, "propemodum ex ipso cœlo petitum." Whoever understands by this merely that the imagination of the artist was fired by the poet's sublime picture, and thus made capable of equally sublime representations, overlooks, I think,

[1] Iliad i. 528. Valerius Maximus, lib. iii. cap. 7.
As thus he spoke the son of Saturn gave
The nod with his dark brows. The ambrosial curls
Upon the Sovereign One's immortal head
Were shaken, and with them the mighty mount
Olympus trembled. — BRYANT.

the chief point, and contents himself with a general statement where something very special and much more satisfactory is meant. Phidias here acknowledges also, as I understand him, that this passage first led him to notice how much expression lies in the eyebrows, "quanta pars animi" is shown in them. Perhaps it further induced him to bestow more attention upon the hair, in order to express in some degree what Homer calls ambrosial curls. For it is certain that the old artists before Phidias had very little idea of the language and significance of the features, and particularly neglected the hair. Even Myron was faulty in both these respects, as Pliny observes,[1] and, according to the same authority, Pythagoras Leontinus was the first who distinguished himself by the beauty of his hair. Other artists learned from the works of Phidias what Phidias had learned from Homer.

I will mention another example of the same kind which has always given me particular pleasure. Hogarth passes the following criticism on the Apollo Belvidere.[2] "These two masterpieces of art, the Apollo and the Antinous, are seen together in the same palace at Rome, where the Antinous fills the spectator with admiration only, whilst the Apollo strikes him with surprise, and, as travellers express themselves, with an appearance of something more than human, which they of course are always at a loss to describe; and this effect, they say, is the more

[1] See Appendix, note 50.

[2] Hogarth's Analysis of Beauty, chap. xi.

astonishing, as, upon examination, its disproportion is evident even to a common eye. One of the best sculptors we have in England, who lately went to see them, confirmed to me what has been now said, particularly as to the legs and thighs being too long and too large for the upper parts. And Andrea Sacchi, one of the great Italian painters, seems to have been of the same opinion, or he would hardly have given his Apollo, crowning Pasquilini the musician, the exact proportion of the Antinous (in a famous picture of his now in England), as otherwise it seems to be a direct copy from the Apollo.

"Although in very great works we often see an inferior part neglected, yet here this cannot be the case, because in a fine statue, just proportion is one of its essential beauties; therefore it stands to reason, that these limbs must have been lengthened on purpose, otherwise it might easily have been avoided.

"So that if we examine the beauties of this figure thoroughly, we may reasonably conclude, that what has been hitherto thought so unaccountably excellent in its general appearance, hath been owing to what hath seemed a blemish in a part of it."

All this is very suggestive. Homer also, I would add, had already felt and noticed the same thing, — that an appearance of nobility is produced by a disproportionate size of the foot and thigh. For, when Antenor is comparing the figure of Ulysses with that of Menelaus, he says,[1] —

[1] Iliad iii. 210.

στάντων μὲν Μενέλαος ὑπείρεχεν εὐρέας ὤμους,
ἄμφω δ' ἑζομένω, γεραρώτερος ἦεν Ὀδυσσεύς.

"When both were standing Menelaus overtopped him by his broad shoulders; but when both were sitting, Ulysses was the more majestic." Since, when seated, Ulysses gained in dignity what Menelaus lost, we can easily tell the proportion which the upper part of the body in each bore to the feet and thighs. In Ulysses the upper part was large in proportion to the lower: in Menelaus the size of the lower parts was large in proportion to that of the upper.

XXIII.

A SINGLE incongruous part may destroy the harmonious effect of many beauties, without, however, making the object ugly. Ugliness requires the presence of several incongruous parts which we must be able to take in at a glance if the effect produced is to be the opposite of that which we call beauty.

Accordingly ugliness in itself can be no subject for poetry. Yet Homer has described its extreme in Thersites, and described it by its coexistent parts. Why did he allow himself in the case of ugliness what he wisely refrained from as regards beauty? Will not the effect of ugliness be as much hindered by the successive enumeration of its elements, as the effect of beauty is neutralized by a similar treatment?

Certainly it will, and therein lies Homer's justification. The poet can make ugliness his theme only because it acquires through his description a less repulsive aspect, and ceases in a measure to produce the effect of ugliness. What he cannot employ by itself, he uses as an ingredient to excite and strengthen certain mixed impressions, with which he must entertain us in the absence of those purely agreeable.

These mixed sensations are those of the ridiculous and the horrible.

Homer makes Thersites ugly in order to make him ridiculous. Mere ugliness, however, would not have this effect. Ugliness is imperfection, and the ridiculous requires a contrast between perfections and imperfections.[1] This is the explanation of my friend, to which I would add that this contrast must not be too sharp and decided, but that the opposites must be such as admit of being blended into each other. All the ugliness of Thersites has not made the wise and virtuous Æsop ridiculous. A silly, monkish conceit sought to transfer to the writer the *γέλοιον* of his instructive fables by representing his person as deformed. But a misshapen body and a beautiful soul are like oil and vinegar, which, however much they may be stirred together, will always remain distinct to the taste. They give rise to no third. Each one produces its own effect, — the body distaste, the soul delight. The two emotions blend into one only when the misshapen body is at the same time frail and sickly, a hinderance and source of injury to the mind. The result, however, is not laughter, but compassion; and the object, which before we had simply respected, now excites our interest. The frail, misshapen Pope must have been more interesting to his friends than the strong, handsome Wycherley.

But although Thersites is not ridiculous on account

[1] Philos. Schriften des Herrn Moses Mendelssohn, vol. ii. p. 23.

of his ugliness alone, he would not be ridiculous without it. Many elements work together to produce this result; the ugliness of his person corresponding with that of his character, and both contrasting with the idea he entertains of his own importance, together with the harmlessness, except to himself, of his malicious tongue. The last point is the *οὐ φθαρτικόν* (the undeadly), which Aristotle[1] takes to be an indispensable element of the ridiculous. My friend also makes it a necessary condition that the contrast should be unimportant, and not interest us greatly. For, suppose that Thersites had had to pay dearly for his spiteful detraction of Agamemnon, that it had cost him his life instead of a couple of bloody wales, then we should cease to laugh at him. To test the justice of this, let us read his death in Quintus Calaber.[2] Achilles regrets having slain Penthesilea. Her noble blood, so bravely shed, claims the hero's respect and compassion, feelings which soon grow into love. The slanderous Thersites turns this love into a crime. He inveighs against the sensuality which betrays even the bravest of men into follies:

ἥτ' ἄφρονα φῶτα τίθησι
καὶ πινυτόν περ ἐόντα.

Achilles' wrath is kindled. Without a word he deals him such a blow between cheek and ear that teeth, blood, and life gush from the wound. This is too barbarous. The angry, murderous Achil-

[1] De Poetica, cap. v. [2] Paralipom. lib. i. 720-778.

les becomes more an object of hate to me than the tricky, snarling Thersites. The shout of delight raised by the Greeks at the deed offends me. My sympathies are with Diomedes, whose sword is drawn on the instant to take vengeance on the murderer of his kinsman. For Thersites as a man is of my kin also.

But suppose that the attempts of Thersites had resulted in open mutiny; that the rebellious people had actually taken to the ships, and treacherously abandoned their commanders, who thereupon had fallen into the hands of a vindictive enemy; and that the judgment of the gods had decreed total destruction to fleet and nation: how should we then view the ugliness of Thersites? Although harmless ugliness may be ridiculous, hurtful ugliness is always horrible.

I cannot better illustrate this than by a couple of admirable passages from Shakespeare. Edmund, bastard son of the Earl of Gloucester in King Lear, is no less a villain than Richard, Duke of Gloucester, who, by the most hideous crimes, paved his way to the throne, which he ascended under the title of Richard the Third. Why does he excite in us far less disgust and horror? When the bastard says,[1] —

> Thou, nature, art my goddess; to thy law
> My services are bound; wherefore should I
> Stand in the plague of custom, and permit
> The curiosity of nations to deprive me,

[1] King Lear, Act i. scene 2.

For that I am some twelve or fourteen moonshines
Lag of a brother? Why bastard? wherefore base?
When my dimensions are as well compact,
My mind as generous, and my shape as true
As honest Madam's issue? why brand they thus
With base? with baseness? bastardy? base, base?
Who, in the lusty stealth of nature, take
More composition and fierce quality,
Than doth, within a dull, stale, tired bed,
Go to creating a whole tribe of fops
Got 'tween asleep and wake?

I hear a devil speaking, but in the form of an angel of light.

When, on the contrary, the Earl of Gloucester says,[1] —

But I, — that am not shaped for sportive tricks,
Nor made to court an amorous looking-glass;
I, that am rudely stamped, and want love's majesty;
To strut before a wanton, ambling nymph;
I, that am curtailed of this fair proportion,
Cheated of feature by dissembling nature,
Deformed, unfinished, sent before my time
Into this breathing world, scarce half made up,
And that so lamely and unfashionably,
That dogs bark at me as I halt by them;
Why I, in this weak piping time of peace,
Have no delight to pass away the time;
Unless to spy my shadow in the sun,
And descant on mine own deformity;
And, therefore, since I cannot prove a lover,
To entertain these fair, well-spoken days,
I am determined to prove a villain.

I hear a devil and see a devil, in a shape which only the devil should wear.

[1] King Richard III. Act i. scene 1.

XXIV.

SUCH is the use which the poet makes of ugliness of form. How can the painter legitimately employ it?

Painting as imitative skill can express ugliness; painting as a fine art will not express it. In the former capacity its sphere extends over all visible objects; in the latter it confines itself to those which produce agreeable impressions.

But do not disagreeable impressions please in the imitation? Not all. An acute critic has already remarked this in respect of disgust.[1] "Representations of fear," he says, "of sadness, horror, compassion, &c., arouse painful emotions only in so far as we believe the evil to be actual. The consideration that it is but an illusion of art may resolve these disagreeable sensations into those of pleasure. But, according to the laws of imagination, the disagreeable sensation of disgust arises from the mere representation in the mind, whether the object be thought actually to exist or not. No matter how apparent the art of the imitation, our wounded sensibilities are not relieved. Our discomfort arose not from the belief that the evil was actual, but from the

[1] Briefe, die neueste Literatur betreffend, Part v. p. 102.

mere representation which is actually present. The feeling of disgust, therefore, comes always from nature, never from imitation."

The same criticism is applicable to physical ugliness. This also wounds our sight, offends our taste for order and harmony, and excites aversion without regard to the actual existence of the object in which we perceive it. We wish to see neither Thersites himself nor his image. If his image be the less displeasing, the reason is not that ugliness of shape ceases to be ugly in the imitation, but that we possess the power of diverting our minds from this ugliness by admiration of the artist's skill. But this satisfaction is constantly disturbed by the thought of the unworthy use to which art has been put, and our esteem for the artist is thereby greatly diminished.

Aristotle adduces another reason[1] for the pleasure we take in even the most faithful copy of what in nature is disagreeable. He attributes this pleasure to man's universal desire for knowledge. We are pleased when we can learn from a copy *τί ἕκαστον*, what each and every thing is, or when we can conclude from it *ὅτι οὗτος ἐκεῖνος*, that it is the very thing we already know. But this is no argument in favor of the imitation of ugliness. The pleasure which arises from the gratification of our desire for knowledge is momentary and only incidental to the object with regard to which it has been satisfied, whereas the discomfort which accompanies the sight of ugli-

[1] De Poetica, cap. iv.

ness is permanent, and essential to the object causing it. How, then, can one counterbalance the other? Still less can the trifling entertainment of tracing a likeness overcome the unpleasant impression produced by ugliness. The more closely I compare the ugly copy with the ugly original, the more I expose myself to this influence, so that the pleasure of the comparison soon disappears, leaving nothing behind but the painful impression of this twofold ugliness.

From the examples given by Aristotle he appears not to include ugliness of form among the disagreeable things which may give pleasure in the imitation. His examples are wild beasts and dead bodies. Wild beasts excite terror even when they are not ugly; and this terror, not their ugliness, may be made to produce sensations of pleasure through imitation. So also of dead bodies. Keenness of sympathy, the dreadful thought of our own annihilation, make a dead body in nature an object of aversion. In the imitation the sense of illusion robs sympathy of its sharpness, and, by the addition of various palliating circumstances, that disturbing element may be either entirely banished or so inseparably interwoven with these softening features, that terror is almost lost in desire.

Since, then, ugliness of form, from its exciting sensations of pain of a kind incapable of being converted by imitation into pleasurable emotions, cannot in itself be a fitting subject for painting as a fine art, the question arises whether it may not be employed in painting as in poetry as an ingredient for strengthening other sensations.

May painting make use of deformity in the attainment of the ridiculous and horrible?

I will not venture to answer this question absolutely in the negative. Unquestionably, harmless ugliness can be ridiculous in painting also, especially when united with an affectation of grace and dignity. Equally beyond question is it that hurtful ugliness excites terror in a picture as well as in nature, and that the ridiculous and the terrible, in themselves mixed sensations, acquire through imitation an added degree of fascination.

But I must call attention to the fact that painting and poetry do not stand upon the same footing in this respect. In poetry, as I have observed, ugliness of form loses its disagreeable effect almost entirely by the successive enumeration of its coexistent parts. As far as effect is concerned it almost ceases to be ugliness, and can thus more closely combine with other appearances to produce new and different impressions. But in painting ugliness is before our eyes in all its strength, and affects us scarcely less powerfully than in nature itself. Harmless ugliness cannot, therefore, long remain ridiculous. The disagreeable impression gains the mastery, and what was at first amusing becomes at last repulsive. Nor is the case different with hurtful ugliness. The element of terror gradually disappears, leaving the deformity unchanging and unrelieved.

Count Caylus was therefore right in omitting the

episode of Thersites from his series of Homeric pictures. But are we justified in wishing it out of Homer? I perceive with regret that this is done by one critic whose taste is otherwise unerring.[1] I postpone further discussion of the subject to a future occasion.

[1] Klotzii Epistolæ Homericæ, p. 33 et seq.

XXV.

THE second distinction mentioned by the critic just quoted, between disgust and other disagreeable emotions, appears in the distaste which deformity excites in us.

"Other disagreeable passions," he says,[1] "may sometimes, in nature as well as in art, produce gratification, because they never arouse pure pain. Their bitterness is always mixed with satisfaction. Our fear is seldom devoid of hope; terror rouses all our powers to escape the danger; anger is mixed with a desire for vengeance; sadness, with the pleasant recollection of former happiness; and compassion is inseparable from the tender sentiments of love and good-will. The mind is at liberty to dwell now on the agreeable, and now on the disagreeable side, and thus to obtain a mingling of pleasure and pain, more delightful than the purest pleasure. Very little study of ourselves will furnish us with abundant instances. Why else is his anger dearer to an angry man and his sadness to a melancholy one, than all the cheerful images by which we strive to soothe him? Quite different is the case with disgust and its kindred sensations. Here the mind is

[1] Klotzii Epistolæ Homericæ, p. 103.

conscious of no perceptible admixture of pleasure. A feeling of uneasiness gains the mastery, and under no imaginable conditions in nature or art would the mind fail to recoil with aversion from representations of this nature."

Very true; but, since the critic acknowledges the existence of other sensations nearly akin to that of disgust, and producing, like that, nothing but pain, what answers more nearly to this description than emotions excited by the sight of physical deformity? These are not only kindred to that of disgust, but they resemble it in being destitute of all admixture of pleasure in art as well as in nature. Under no imaginable conditions, therefore, would the mind fail to recoil with aversion from such representations.

This aversion, if I have analyzed my feelings with sufficient care, is altogether of the nature of disgust. The sensation which accompanies the sight of physical deformity is disgust, though a low degree of it. This, indeed, is at variance with another remark of our critic, according to which only our more occult senses — those of taste, smell, and touch — are capable of receiving impressions of disgust. "The first two," he says, "from an excessive sweetness, and the latter from an extreme softness of bodies which offer too slight resistance to the fibres coming in contact with them. Such objects, then, become intolerable to the sight, but solely through the association of ideas, because we remember how disagreeable they were to our sense of taste, smell, or touch.

For, strictly speaking, there are no objects of disgust to the eyes." I think, however, that some might be mentioned. A mole on the face, a hare-lip, a flattened nose with prominent nostrils, are deformities which offend neither taste, smell, nor touch. Yet the sight of them excites in us something much more nearly resembling disgust than we feel at sight of other malformations, such as a club-foot or a hump on the back. The more susceptible the temperament, the more distinctly are we conscious, when looking at such objects, of those motions in the body which precede nausea. That these motions soon subside, and rarely if ever result in actual sickness, is to be explained by the fact that the eye receives in and with the objects causing them such a number of pleasing images that the disagreeable impressions are too much weakened and obscured to exert any marked influence on the body. The more occult senses of taste, smell, and touch, on the contrary, cannot receive other impressions when in contact with the repulsive object. The element of disgust operates in full force, and necessarily produces much more violent effects upon the body.

The same rules hold of things loathsome as of things ugly, in respect of imitation. Indeed, since the disagreeable effect of the former is the more violent, they are still less suitable subjects of painting or poetry. Only because the effect is softened by verbal expression, did I venture to assert that the poet might employ certain loathsome traits as an ingredient in such mixed sensations as can with good effect be strengthened by the use of ugliness.

The ridiculous may be heightened by an element of disgust; representations of dignity and propriety likewise become ludicrous when brought into contrast with the disgusting. Examples of this abound in Aristophanes. I am reminded of the weasel that interrupted the worthy Socrates in his astronomical observations.[1]

> *ΜΑΘ. πρώην δέ γε γνώμην μεγάλην ἀφῃρέθη*
> *ὑπ' ἀσκαλαβώτου. ΣΤΡ. τίνα τρόπον; κάτειπέ μοι.*
> *ΜΑΘ. ζητοῦντος αὐτοῦ τῆς σελήνης τὰς ὁδοὺς*
> *καὶ τὰς περιφοράς, εἶτ' ἄνω κεχηνότος*
> *ἀπὸ τῆς ὀροφῆς νύκτωρ γαλεώτης κατέχεσεν.*
> *ΣΤΡ. ἥσθην γαλεώτῃ καταχέσαντι Σωκράτους.*

If what fell into the open mouth had not been disgusting, there would be nothing ludicrous in the story.

An amusing instance of this occurs in the Hottentot story of Tquassouw and Knonmquaiha, attributed to Lord Chesterfield, which appeared in the "Connoisseur," an English weekly, full of wit and humor. The filthiness of the Hottentots is well known, as also the fact of their regarding as beautiful and holy what excites our disgust and aversion. The pressed gristle of a nose, flaccid breasts descend-

[1] Nubes, 170–174. *Disciple.* But he was lately deprived of a great idea by a weasel. *Strepsiades.* In what way? tell me. *Disciple.* He was studying the courses of the moon and her revolutions, and, while gazing upward open-mouthed, a weasel in the dark dunged upon him from the roof.

ing to the navel, the whole body anointed with a varnish of goat's fat and soot, melted in by the sun, hair dripping with grease, arms and legs entwined with fresh entrails, — imagine all this the object of an ardent, respectful, tender love; listen to expressions of this love in the noble language of sincerity and admiration, and keep from laughing if you can.[1]

The disgusting seems to admit of being still more closely united with the terrible. What we call the horrible is nothing more than a mixture of the elements of terror and disgust. Longinus[2] takes offence at the *Τῆς ἐκ μὲν ῥινῶν μύξαι ῥεόν* (mucus flowing from the nostrils) in Hesiod's picture of Sorrow;[3] but not, I think, so much on account of the loathsomeness of the trait, as from its being simply loathsome with no element of terror. For he does not seem inclined to find fault with the *μακροὶ δ' ὄνυχες χείρεσσιν ὑπῆσαν*, the long nails projecting beyond the fingers. Long nails are not less disgusting than a running nose, but they are at the same time terrible. It is they that tear the cheeks till the blood runs to the ground:

> . . . ἐκ δὲ παρειῶν
> αἷμ' ἀπελείβετ' ἔραζε . . .

The other feature is simply disgusting, and I should advise Sorrow to cease her crying.

[1] See Appendix, note 51.

[2] Περὶ Ὕψους, τμῆμα ή. p. 15 (edit. T. Fabri).

[3] Scut. Hercul. 266.

Read Sophocles' description of the desert cave of his wretched Philoctetes. There are no provisions to be seen, no comforts beyond a trampled litter of dried leaves, an unshapely wooden bowl, and a tinder-box. These constitute the whole wealth of the sick, forsaken man. How does the poet complete the sad and frightful picture? By introducing the element of disgust. "Ha!" Neoptolemus draws back of a sudden, "here are rags drying full of blood and matter." [1]

> *ΝΕ.* ὁρῶ κενὴν οἴκησιν ἀνθρώπων δίχα.
> *ΟΔ.* οὐδ' ἔνδον οἰκοποιός ἐστί τις τροφή;
> *ΝΕ.* στείπτή γε φυλλὰς ὡς ἐναυλίζοντί τῳ.
> *ΟΔ.* τὰ δ' ἄλλ' ἔρημα, κοὔδέν ἐσθ' ὑπόστεγον;
> *ΝΕ.* αὐτόξυλόν γ' ἔκπωμα φαυλουργοῦ τινὸς
> τεχνήματ' ἀνδρὸς, καὶ πυρεῖ' ὁμοῦ τάδε.
> *ΟΔ.* κείνου τὸ θησαύρισμα σημαίνεις τόδε.
> *ΝΕ.* ἰοὺ, ἰού· καὶ ταῦτά γ' ἄλλα θάλπεται
> ῥάκη, βαρείας του νοσηλείας πλέα.

So in Homer, Hector dragged on the ground, his face foul with dust, his hair matted with blood,

> Squalentem barbam et concretos sanguine crines,

(as Virgil expresses it [2]) is a disgusting object, but all the more terrible and touching.

Who can recall the punishment of Marsyas, in Ovid, without a feeling of disgust? [3]

[1] Philoct. 31–39.

[2] Æneid, lib. ii. 277.

[3] Metamorph. vi. 387. "The skin is torn from the upper limbs of the shrieking Marsyas, till he is nought but one great wound: thick blood oozes on every side; the bared sinews are

> Clamanti cutis est summos direpta per artus:
> Nec quidquam, nisi vulnus erat; cruor undique manat:
> Detectique patent nervi: trepidæque sine ulla
> Pelle micant venæ: salientia viscera possis,
> Et perlucentes numerare in pectore fibras.

But the loathsome details are here appropriate. They make the terrible horrible, which in fiction is far from displeasing to us; since, even in nature, where our compassion is enlisted, things horrible are not wholly devoid of charm.

I do not wish to multiply examples, but this one thing I must further observe. There is one form of the horrible, the road to which lies almost exclusively through the disgusting, and that is the horror of famine. Even in ordinary life we can convey no idea of extreme hunger save by enumerating all the innutritious, unwholesome, and particularly disgusting things with which the stomach would fain appease its cravings. Since imitation can excite nothing of the feeling of actual hunger, it has recourse to another disagreeable sensation which, in cases of extreme hunger, is felt to be a lesser evil. We may thus infer how intense that other suffering must be which makes the present discomfort in comparison of small account.

Ovid says of the Oread whom Ceres sent to meet Famine,[1] —

visible; and the palpitating veins quiver, stripped of the covering of skin; you can count the protruding entrails, and the muscles shining in the breast.

[1] Metamorph. lib. viii. 809. "Seeing Famine afar off, she delivers the message of the goddess. And after a little

Hanc (Famem) procul ut vidit. . . .
. . . refert mandata deæ; paulumque morata
Quanquam aberat longe, quanquam modo venerat illuc,
Visa tamen sensisse famem . . .

This is an unnatural exaggeration. The sight of a hungry person, even of Hunger herself, has no such power of contagion. Compassion and horror and loathing may be aroused, but not hunger. Ovid has not been sparing of this element of the horrible in the picture of Famine; while both he and Callimachus,[1] in their description of Erisichthon's starvation, have laid chief emphasis upon the loathsome traits. After Erisichthon has devoured every thing, not sparing even the sacrificial cow, which his mother had been fattening for Vesta, Callimachus makes him fall on horses and cats, and beg in the streets for crumbs and filthy refuse from other men's tables.

Καὶ τὰν βῶν ἔφαγεν, τὰν Ἑστίᾳ ἔτρεφε μάτηρ,
Καὶ τὸν ἀεθλόφορον καὶ τὸν πολεμήιον ἵππον,
Καὶ τὰν αἴλουρον, τὰν ἔτρεμε θήρια μικκά—
Καὶ τόθ' ὁ τῶ βασιλῆος ἐνὶ τριόδοισι καθῆστο
αἰτίζων ἀκόλως τε καὶ ἔκβολα λύματα δαιτός.

Ovid represents him finally as biting into his own flesh, that his body might thus furnish nourishment for itself.

Vis tamen illa mali postquam consumserat omnem
Materiam . . .
Ipse suos artus lacero divellere morsu
Cœpit · et infelix minuendo corpus alebat.

while, although she was yet at a distance and was but approaching, yet the mere sight produced hunger."

[1] Hym. in Cererem, 111–116.

The hideous harpies were made loathsome and obscene in order that the hunger occasioned by their carrying off of the food might be the more horrible. Hear the complaints of Phineus in Apollonius:[1] —

> *τυτθὸν δ' ἤν ἄρα δή ποτ' ἐδητύος ἄμμι λίπωσι,*
> *πνεῖ τόδε μυδαλέον τε καὶ οὐ τλητὸν μένος ὀδμῆς.*
> *οὔ κὲ τις οὐδὲ μίνυνθα βρότων ἄνσχοιτο πελάσσας,*
> *οὐδ' εἰ οἱ ἀδάμαντος ἐληλαμένον κέαρ εἴη.*
> *ἀλλά με πικρὴ δῆτά κε δαῖτος ἐπίσχει ἀνάγκη*
> *μίμνειν, καὶ μίμνοντα κακῇ ἐν γαστέρι θέσθαι.*

I would gladly excuse in this way, if I could, Virgil's disgusting introduction of the harpies. They, however, instead of occasioning an actual present hunger, only prophesy an inward craving; and this prophecy, moreover, is resolved finally into a mere play upon words.

Dante not only prepares us for the starvation of Ugolino by a most loathsome, horrible description of him together with his former persecutor in hell, but the slow starvation itself is not free from disgusting features, as where the sons offer themselves as food for the father. I give in a note a passage from a play by Beaumont and Fletcher, which might have served me in the stead of all other examples, were it not somewhat too highly drawn.[2]

[1] Argonaut. lib. ii. 228–233. "Scarcely have they left us any food that smells not mouldy, and the stench is unendurable. No one for a time could bear the foul food, though his stomach were beaten of adamant. But bitter necessity compels me to bethink me of the meal, and, so remembering, put it into my wretched belly"

[2] See Appendix, note 52.

I come now to objects of disgust in painting. Even could we prove that there are no objects directly disgusting to the eye, which painting as a fine art would naturally avoid, it would still be obliged to refrain from loathsome objects in general, because they become through the association of ideas disgusting also to the sense of sight. Pordenone, in a picture of the entombment, makes one of the bystanders hold his nose. Richardson[1] objects to this on the ground that Christ had not been long enough dead for corruption to set in. In the raising of Lazarus, however, he would allow the painter to represent some of the lookers-on in that attitude, because the narrative expressly states that the body was already offensive. But I consider the representation in both cases as insufferable, for not only the actual smell, but the very idea of it is nauseous. We shun bad-smelling places even when we have a cold in the head. But painting does not employ loathsomeness for its own sake, but, like poetry, to give emphasis to the ludicrous and the terrible. At its peril! What I have already said of ugliness in this connection applies with greater force to loathsomeness. This also loses much less of its effect in a visible representation than in a description addressed to the ear, and can therefore unite less closely with the elements of the ludicrous and terrible in painting than in poetry. As soon as the surprise passes and the first curious glance is satisfied, the elements separate and loathsomeness appears in all its crudity.

[1] Richardson de la Peinture, vol. i. p. 74.

XXVI.

WINKELMANN'S "History of Ancient Art" has appeared, and I cannot venture a step further until I have read it. Criticism based solely upon general principles may lead to conceits which sooner or later we find to our shame refuted in works on art.

The ancients well understood the connection between painting and poetry, and are sure not to have drawn the two arts more closely together than the good of both would warrant. What their artists have done will teach me what artists in general should do; and where such a man precedes with the torch of history, speculation may boldly follow.

We are apt to turn over the leaves of an important work before seriously setting ourselves to read it. My chief curiosity was to know the author's opinion of the Laocoon; not of its merit as a work of art, for that he had already given, but merely of its antiquity. Would he agree with those who think that Virgil had the group before him, or with those who suppose the sculptors to have followed the poet?

I am pleased to find that he says nothing of

imitation on either side. What need is there, indeed, of supposing imitation?

Very possibly the resemblances which I have been considering between the poetic picture and the marble group were not intentional but accidental, and, so far from one having served as a model for the other, the two may not even have had a common model. Had he, however, been misled by an appearance of imitation, he must have declared in favor of those who make Virgil the imitator. For he supposes the Laocoon to date from the period when Greek art was in its perfection: to be, therefore, of the time of Alexander the Great.

"Kind fortune," he says,[1] "watching over the arts even in their extinction, has preserved for the admiration of the world a work of this period of art, which proves the truth of what history tells concerning the glory of the many lost masterpieces. The Laocoon with his two sons, the work of Agesander, Apollodorus,[2] and Athenodorus, of Rhodes, dates in all probability from this period, although we cannot determine the exact time, nor give, as some have done, the Olympiad in which these artists flourished."

In a note he adds: "Pliny says not a word with

1 Geschichte der Kunst, p. 347.

2 Not Apollodorus, but Polydorus. Pliny is the only one who mentions these artists, and I am not aware that the manuscripts differ in the writing of the name. Had such been the case, Hardouin would certainly have noticed it. All the older editions also read Polydorus. Winkelmann must therefore have merely made a slight error in transcribing

regard to the time when Agesander and his assistants lived. But Maffei, in his explanation of the ancient statues, professes to know that these artists flourished in the eighty-eighth Olympiad; and others, like Richardson, have maintained the same on his authority. He must, I think, have mistaken an Athenodorus, a pupil of Polycletus, for one of our artists. Polycletus flourished in the eighty-seventh Olympiad, and his supposed pupil was therefore referred to the Olympiad following. Maffei can have no other grounds for his opinion."

Certainly he can have no other. But why does Winkelmann content himself with the mere mention of this supposed argument of Maffei? Does it refute itself? Not altogether. For although not otherwise supported, it yet carries with it a certain degree of probability unless we can prove that Athenodorus, the pupil of Polycletus, and Athenodorus, the assistant of Agesander and Polydorus, could not possibly have been one and the same person. Happily this is proved by the fact that the two were natives of different countries. We have the express testimony of Pausanias[1] that the first Athenodorus was from Clitor in Arcadia, while the second, on the authority of Pliny, was born at Rhodes.

Winkelmann can have had no object in refraining from a direct refutation of Maffei by the statement of this circumstance. Probably the arguments which

[1] Ἀθηνοδῶρος δὲ καὶ Δαμίας . . . οὗτοι δὲ Ἀρκάδες εἰσιν ἐκ Κλειτόρος. Phoc cap. ix. p 819 (edit. Kuhn).

his undoubted critical knowledge derived from the skill of the workmanship seemed to him of such great weight, that he deemed any slight probability which Maffei's opinion might have on its side a matter of no importance. He doubtless recognized in the Laocoon too many of those *argutiæ*[1] (traits of animation) peculiar to Lysippus, to suppose it to be of earlier date than that master who was the first to enrich art with this semblance of life.

But, granting the fact to be proved that the Laocoon cannot be older than Lysippus, have we thereby proved that it must be contemporaneous with him or nearly so? May it not be a work of much later date? Passing in review those periods previous to the rise of the Roman monarchy, when art in Greece alternately rose and sank, why, I ask, might not Laocoon have been the happy fruit of that emulation which the extravagant luxury of the first emperors must have kindled among artists? Why might not Agesander and his assistants have been the contemporaries of Strongylion, Arcesilaus, Pasiteles, Posidonius, or Diogenes? Were not some of the works of those masters counted among the greatest treasures ever produced by art? And if undoubted works from the hand of these men were still in existence, but the time in which they lived was unknown and left to be determined by the style of their art, would not some inspiration from heaven be needed to prevent the critic from refer-

[1] Plinius, lib. xxxiv. sect. 19.

ring them to that period which to Winkelmann seemed the only one worthy of producing the Laocoon?

Pliny, it is true, does not expressly mention the time when the sculptors of the Laocoon lived. But were I to conclude from a study of the whole passage whether he would have them reckoned among the old or the new artists, I confess the probability seems to me in favor of the latter inference. Let the reader judge.

After speaking at some length of the oldest and greatest masters of sculpture, — Phidias, Praxiteles, and Scopas, — and then giving, without chronological order, the names of the rest, especially of those who were represented in Rome by any of their works Pliny proceeds as follows:[1] —

[1] Lib. xxxvi. sect. 4. "Nor are there many of great repute the number of artists engaged on celebrated works preventing the distinction of individuals; since no one could have all the credit, nor could the names of many be rehearsed at once: as in the Laocoon, which is in the palace of the emperor Titus, a work surpassing all the results of painting or statuary. From one stone he and his sons and the wondrous coils of the serpents were sculptured by consummate artists, working in concert: Agesander, Polydorus, and Athenodorus, all of Rhodes. In like manner Craterus with Pythodorus, Polydectes with Hermolaus, another Pythodorus with Artemon, and Aphrodisius of Tralles by himself, filled the palaces of the Cæsars on the Palatine with admirable statuary. Diogenes, the Athenian, decorated the Pantheon of Agrippa, and the Caryatides on the columns of that temple rank among the choicest works, as do also the statues on the pediment, though these, from the height of their position, are less celebrated."

Nec multo plurium fama est, quorundam claritati in operibus eximiis obstante numero artificum, quoniam nec unus occupat gloriam, nec plures pariter nuncupari possunt, sicut in Laocoonte, qui est in Titi Imperatoris domo, opus omnibus et picturæ et statuariæ artis præponendum. Ex uno lapide eum et liberos draconumque mirabiles nexus de consilii sententia fecere summi artifices, Agesander et Polydorus et Athenodorus Rhodii. Similiter Palatinas domus Cæsarum replevere probatissimis signis Craterus cum Pythodoro, Polydectes cum Hermolao, Pythodorus alius cum Artemone, et singularis Aphrodisius Trallianus. Agrippæ Pantheum decoravit Diogenes Atheniensis; et Caryatides in columnis templi ejus probantur inter pauca operum: sicut in fastigio posita signa, sed propter altitudinem loci minus celebrata.

Of all the artists mentioned in this passage, Diogenes of Athens is the one whose date is fixed with the greatest precision. He adorned the Pantheon of Agrippa, and therefore lived under Augustus. But a close examination of Pliny's words will, I think, determine with equal certainty the date of Craterus and Pythodorus, Polydectes and Hermolaus, the second Pythodorus and Artemon, as also of Aphrodisius of Tralles. He says of them: "Palatinas domus Cæsarum replevere probatissimis signis." Can this mean only that the palaces were filled with admirable works by these artists, which the emperors had collected from various places and brought to their dwellings in Rome? Surely not. The sculptors must have executed their works expressly for the imperial palaces, and must, therefore, have lived at the time of these emperors. That they were artists of comparatively late date, who worked only in Italy, is plain from our finding no mention of them elsewhere. Had they worked in Greece at an earlier day, Pausanias would have seen some work of theirs and recorded it. He mentions, indeed, a Pythodorus,[1] but Hardouin is wrong in supposing him to be the same referred to by Pliny. For Pausanias calls the statue of Juno at Coronæa, in Bœotia, the work of the former, *ἄγαλμα ἀρχαῖον* (an ancient idol), a term which he applies only to the works of those artists who lived in the first rude days of art, long before Phidias and Praxiteles. With such works the emperors would certainly not have adorned their palaces. Of still less value is another suggestion of Hardouin, that Artemon may be the painter of the same name elsewhere mentioned by Pliny. Identity of name is a slight argument, and by no means authorizes us to do violence to the natural interpretation of an uncorrupted passage.

If it be proved beyond a doubt that Craterus and Pythodorus, Polydectes and Hermolaus, with the rest, lived at the time of the emperors whose palaces they adorned with their admirable works, then I think we can assign no other date to those artists, the sculptors of the Laocoon, whose names Pliny connects with these by the word *similiter*. For if Agesander, Polydorus, and Athenodorus were really such old masters as Winkelmann supposes, it would be the height of impropriety for an author, who makes great account of precision of expression, to

[1] Bœotic. cap. xxxiv. p. 778 (edit. Kuhn).

leap from them to the most modern artists, merely with the words "in like manner."

But it may be urged that this *similiter* has no reference to a common date, but to some other circumstance common to all these masters, who yet in age were widely different. Pliny, it may be said, is speaking of artists who had worked in partnership, and on this account had not obtained the fame they merited. The names of all had been left in neglect, because no one artist could appropriate the honor of the common work, and to mention the names of all the participators would require too much time (quoniam nec unus occupat gloriam, nec plures pariter nuncupari possunt). This had been the fate of the sculptors of the Laocoon, as well as of the many other masters whom the emperors had employed in the decoration of their palaces.

But, granting all this, the probabilities are still in favor of the supposition that Pliny meant to refer only to the later artists whose labors had been in common. If he had meant to include older ones, why confine himself to the sculptors of the Laocoon?

Why not mention others, as Onatas and Calliteles, Timocles and Timarchides, or the sons of this Timarchides, who together had made a statue of Jupiter at Rome?[1] Winkelmann himself says that a long list might be made of older works which had more than one father.[2] And would Pliny have thought but of the single example of Agesander, Polydorus, and

[1] Plinius, lib. xxxvi. sect. 4, p. 730.

[2] Geschichte der Kunst, part ii. p. 331.

Athenodorus, if he had not meant to confine himself strictly to the more modern masters?

If ever a conjecture gained in probability from the number and magnitude of the difficulties solved by it, this one, that the sculptors of the Laocoon flourished under the first emperors, has that advantage in a high degree. For had they lived and worked in Greece at the time which Winkelmann assigns to them, had the Laocoon itself existed earlier in Greece, then the utter silence of the Greeks with regard to such a work, "surpassing all the results of painting or statuary" (opere omnibus et picturæ et statuariæ artis præponendo), is most surprising. It is hard to believe that such great masters should have created nothing else, or that the rest of their works should have been, equally with the Laocoon, unknown to Pausanias. In Rome, on the contrary, the greatest masterpiece might have remained long concealed. If the Laocoon had been finished as early as the time of Augustus, there would be nothing surprising in Pliny's being the first, and, indeed, the last, to mention it. For remember what he tells[1] of a Venus by Scopas, which stood in the temple of Mars at Rome:

. . . "quemcunque alium locum nobilitatura. Romæ quidem magnitudo operum eam obliterat, ac magni officiorum negotiorumque acervi omnes a contemplatione talium abducunt: quoniam otiosorum et in magno loci silentio apta admiratio talis est."

[1] Plinius, xxxvi. sect. 4. . . . "which would make the glory of any other place. But at Rome the greatness of other works overshadows it, and the great press of business and engagements turns the crowd from the contemplation of such things; for the admiration of works of art belongs to those who have leisure and great quiet."

Those who would fain see in the group an imitation of Virgil's Laocoon will readily catch at what I have been saying, nor will they be displeased at another conjecture which just occurs to me. Why should not Asinius Pollio, they may think, have been the patron who had Virgil's Laocoon put into marble by Greek artists? Pollio was a particular friend of the poet, survived him, and appears to have written an original work on the Æneid. For whence but from such a work could the various comments have been drawn which Servius quotes from that author?[1] Pollio was, moreover, a lover of art and a connoisseur, possessed a valuable collection of the best of the old masterpieces, ordered new works from the artists of his day, and showed in his choice a taste quite likely to be pleased by so daring a piece as the Laocoon,[2] "ut fuit acris vehementiæ, sic quoque spectari monumenta sua voluit."

Since, however, the cabinet of Pollio in Pliny's day, when the Laocoon was standing in the palace of Titus, seems to have existed entire in a separate building, this supposition again loses something of its probability. Why might not Titus himself have done what we are trying to ascribe to Pollio?

[1] See Appendix, note 53. [2] Plinius, xxxvi. sect. 4.

XXVII.

A LITTLE item first brought to my notice by Winkelmann himself confirms me in my opinion that the sculptors of the Laocoon lived at the time of the emperors, or at least could not date from so early a period as he assigns them. It is this:[1] "In Nettuno, the ancient Antium, Cardinal Alexander Albani discovered in 1717 in a deep vault, which lay buried under the sea, a vase of the grayish black marble now called *bigio*, wherein the Laocoon was inlaid. Upon this vase is the following inscription:—

ΑΘΑΝΟΔΩΡΟΣ ΑΓΗΣΑΝΔΡΟΥ
ΡΟΔΙΟΣ ΕΠΟΙΗΣΕ.

"Athanadorus of Rhodes, son of Agesander, made it." We learn from this inscription that father and son worked on the Laocoon; and probably Apollodorus (Polydorus) was also a son of Agesander, for this Athanodorus can be no other than the one mentioned by Pliny. The inscription also proves that more than three works of art have been found — the number stated by Pliny — on which the artists have set the word "made," in definite past time, ἐποίησε, *fecit.*

[1] Geschichte der Kunst, part ii. p. 347.

Other artists, he says, from modesty, made use of indefinite time, "was making," *ἐποίει*, *faciebat*.

Few will contradict Winkelmann in his conclusion that the Athanodorus of this inscription can be no other than the Athenodorus whom Pliny mentions as among the sculptors of the Laocoon. Athanodorus and Athenodorus are entirely synonymous; for the Rhodians used the Doric dialect. But the other conclusions which he draws from the inscription require further comment.

The first, that Athenodorus was a son of Agesander, may pass. It is highly probable, though by no means certain. Some of the old artists, we know, called themselves after their teachers instead of taking their fathers' names. What Pliny says of the brothers Apollonius and Tauriscus cannot well be explained in any other way.[1]

But shall we say that this inscription contradicts the statement of Pliny that there were only three works of art to which their masters had set their names in definite past time (*ἐποίησε* instead of *ἐποίει*)? This inscription! What need of this to teach us what we might have learned long ago from a multitude of others? On the statue of Germanicus was there not the inscription *Κλεομένης — ἐποίησε*, Cleomenes made? on the so-called Apotheosis of Homer, *Ἀρχέλαος ἐποίησε*, Archelaus made? on the well-known vase at Gaeta, *Σαλπίων ἐποίησε*, Salpion made? nor are other instances wanting.[2]

[1] Lib. xxxvi. sect. 4.

[2] See Appendix, note 54.

Winkelmann may answer: "No one knows that better than I. So much the worse for Pliny. His statement has been so much the oftener contradicted, and is so much the more surely refuted."

By no means. How if Winkelmann has made Pliny say more than he meant to say? How if these examples contradict, not Pliny's statement, but only something which Winkelmann supposes him to have stated? And this is actually the case. I must quote the whole passage. Pliny, in the dedication of his work to Titus, speaks with the modesty of a man who knows better than any one else how far what he has accomplished falls short of perfection. He finds a noteworthy example of such modesty among the Greeks, on the ambitious and boastful titles of whose books (inscriptiones, propter quas vadimonium deseri possit) he dwells at some length, and then says:[1]

[1] Prefatio Edit. Sillig. "Lest I should seem to find too much fault with the Greeks, I would be classed with those founders of the art of painting and sculpture, recorded in these little volumes, whose works, although complete and such as cannot be sufficiently admired, yet bear a suspended title, as Apelles or Polycletus 'was making'; as if the work were always only begun and still incomplete, so that the artist might appeal from criticism as if himself desirous of improving, had he not been interrupted. Wherefore from modesty they inscribed every work as if it had been their last, and in hand at their death. I think there are but three with the inscription, 'He made it,' and these I shall speak of in their place. From this it appeared that the artists felt fully satisfied with their work, and these excited the envy of all."

Et ne in totum videar Græcos insectari, ex illis nos velim intelligi pingendi fingendique conditoribus, quos in libellis his invenies, absoluta opera, et illa quoque quæ mirando non satiamur, pendenti titulo inscripsisse: ut APELLES FACIEBAT, aut POLYCLETUS: tanquam inchoata semper arte et imperfecta: ut contra judiciorum varietates superesset artifici regressus ad veniam, velut emendaturo quidquid desideraretur, si non esset interceptus. Quare plenum verecundiæ illud est, quod omnia opera tanquam novissima inscripsere, et tanquam singulis fato adempti. Tria non amplius, ut opinor, absolute traduntur inscripta, ILLE FECIT, quæ suis locis reddam: quo apparuit, summam artis securitatem auctori placuisse, et ob id magna invidia fuere omnia ea.

I desire to call particular attention to the words of Pliny, "pingendi fingendique conditoribus" (the creators of the imitative arts). Pliny does not say that it was the habit of all artists of every date to affix their names to their works in indefinite past time. He says explicitly that only the first of the old masters — those creators of the imitative arts, Apelles, Polycletus, and their contemporaries — possessed this wise modesty, and, by his mention of these alone, he gives plainly to be understood, though he does not actually say it in words, that their successors, particularly those of a late date, expressed themselves with greater assurance.

With this interpretation, which is the only true one, we may fully accept the inscription from the hand of one of the three sculptors of the Laocoon without impugning the truth of what Pliny says, that but three works existed whereon their creators had cut the inscription in the finished past time; only three, that is, among all the older works, of the time of Apelles, Polycletus, Nicias, and Lysippus. But then we cannot accept the conclusion that Athenodorus and his assistants were contemporaries of Apelles and Lysippus, as Winkelmann would make them. We should reason thus. If it be true that among the works of the old masters, Apelles, Polycletus, and others of that class, there were but three whose inscriptions stood in definite past time, and if it be further true that Pliny has mentioned these three by name,[1] then Athenodorus, who had made neither of these three works, and who nevertheless employs the definite past time in his inscriptions, cannot belong among those old masters; he cannot be a contemporary of Apelles and Lysippus, but must have a later date assigned him.

In short, we may, I think, take it as a safe criterion that all artists who employed the *ἐποίησε*, the definite past tense, flourished long after the time of Alexander the Great, either under the empire or shortly before. Of Cleomenes this is unquestionably true; highly probable of Archelaus; and of Salpion the contrary, at least, cannot be proved. So also of the rest, not excepting Athenodorus.

Let Winkelmann himself decide. But I protest beforehand against the converse of the proposition. If all who employed the *ἐποίησε* belong among the later artists, not all who have used the *ἐποίει* are to be reckoned among the earliest. Some of the more recent artists also may have really possessed this becoming modesty, and by others it may have been assumed.

[1] See Appendix, note 55.

XXVIII.

NEXT to his judgment of the Laocoon, I was curious to know what Winkelmann would say of the so-called Borghese Gladiator. I think I have made a discovery with regard to this statue, and I rejoice in it with all a discoverer's delight.

I feared lest Winkelmann should have anticipated me, but there is nothing of the kind in his work. If ought could make me doubt the correctness of my conjecture, it would be the fact that my alarm was uncalled for.

"Some critics," says Winkelmann,[1] "take this statue for that of a discobolus, that is, of a person throwing a disc or plate of metal. This opinion was expressed by the famous Herr von Stosch in a paper addressed to me. But he cannot have sufficiently studied the position which such a figure would assume. A person in the act of throwing must incline his body backward, with the weight upon the right thigh, while the left leg is idle. Here the contrary is the case. The whole figure is thrown forward, and rests on the left thigh while the right leg is stretched backward to its full extent. The right arm is new, and a piece of a lance has been placed in the hand. On

[1] Geschichte der Kunst, part i. p. 394.

the left can be seen the strap that held the shield The fact that the head and eyes are turned upward and that the figure seems to be protecting himself with the shield against some danger from above would rather lead us to consider this statue as representing a soldier who had especially distinguished himself in some position of peril. The Greeks probably never paid their gladiators the honor of erecting them a statue; and this work, moreover, seems to have been made previous to the introduction of gladiators into Greece."

The criticism is perfectly just. The statue is no more a gladiator than it is a discobolus, but really represents a soldier who distinguished himself in this position on occasion of some great danger. After this happy guess, how could Winkelmann help going a step further? Why did he not think of that warrior who in this very attitude averted the destruction of a whole army, and to whom his grateful country erected a statue in the same posture?

The statue, in short, is Chabrias.

This is proved by the following passage from Nepos' life of that commander: —[1]

[1] Cap. i. "He was also reckoned among their greatest leaders, and did many things worthy of being remembered. Among his most brilliant achievements was his device in the battle which took place near Thebes, when he had come to the aid of the Bœotians. For when the great leader Agesilaus was now confident of victory, and his own hired troops had fled he would not surrender the remainder of the phalanx, but with knee braced against his shield and lance thrust forward, he taught his men to receive the attack of the enemy. At

"Hic quoque in summis habitus est ducibus; resque multas memoria dignas gessit. Sed ex his elucet maxime inventum ejus in prœlio, quod apud Thebas fecit, quum Bœotiis subsidio venisset. Namque in eo victoriæ fidente summo duce Agesilao, fugatis jam ab eo conductitiis catervis, reliquam phalangem loco vetuit cedere, obnixoque genu scuto, projectaque hasta impetum excipere hostium docuit. Id novum Agesilaus contuens, progredi non est ausus suosque jam incurrentes tuba revocavit. Hoc usque eo tota Græcia fama celebratum est, ut illo statu Chabrias sibi statuam fieri voluerit, quæ publice ei ab Atheniensibus in foro constituta est. Ex quo factum est, ut postea athletæ, ceterique artifices his statibus in statuis ponendis uterentur in quibus victoriam essent adepti."

The reader will hesitate a moment, I know, before yielding his assent; but, I hope, only for a moment. The attitude of Chabrias appears to be not exactly that of the Borghese statue. The thrusting forward of the lance, "projecta hasta," is common to both; but commentators explain the "obnixo genu scuto" to be "obnixo genu in scutum," "obfirmato genu ad scutum." Chabrias is supposed to have showed his men how to brace the knee against the shield and await the enemy behind this bulwark, whereas the statue holds the shield aloft. But what if the commentators are wrong, and instead of "obnixo genu scuto" belong-

sight of this new spectacle, Agesilaus feared to advance, and ordered the trumpet to recall his men who were already advancing. This became famous through all Greece, and Chabrias wished that a statue should be erected to him in this position, which was set up at the public cost in the forum at Athens. Whence it happened that afterwards athletes and other artists [or persons versed in some art] had statues erected to them in the same position in which they had obtained victory."

ing together, "obnixo genu" were meant to be read by itself and "scuto" alone, or in connection with the "projectaque hasta," which follows? The insertion of a single comma makes the correspondence perfect. The statue is a soldier, "qui obnixo genu,[1] scuto projectaque hasta impetum hostis excipit," who, with firmly set knee, and shield and lance advanced, awaits the approach of the enemy. It shows what Chabrias did, and is the statue of Chabrias. That a comma belongs here is proved by the "que" affixed to the "projecta," which would be superfluous if "obnixo genu scuto" belonged together, and has, therefore, been actually omitted in some editions.

The great antiquity which this interpretation assigns to the statue is confirmed by the shape of the letters in the inscription. These led Winkelmann himself to the conclusion that this was the oldest of the statues at present existing in Rome on which the master had written his name. I leave it to his critical eye to detect, if possible, in the style of the workmanship any thing which conflicts with my opinion. Should he bestow his approval, I may flatter myself on having furnished a better example than is to be found in Spence's whole folio of the happy manner in which the classic authors can be explained by the old masterpieces, and in turn throw light upon them.

[1] See Appendix, note 56.

XXIX.

WINKELMANN has brought to his work, together with immense reading and an extensive and subtle knowledge of art, that noble confidence of the old masters which led them to devote all their attention to the main object, treating all secondary matters with what seems like studied neglect, or abandoning them altogether to any chance hand.

A man may take no little credit to himself for having committed only such errors as anybody might have avoided. They force themselves upon our notice at the first hasty reading; and my only excuse for commenting on them is that I would remind a certain class of persons, who seem to think no one has eyes but themselves, that they are trifles not worthy of comment.

In his writings on the imitation of the Greek works of art, Winkelmann had before allowed himself to be misled by Junius, who is, indeed, a very deceptive author. His whole work is a cento, and since his rule is to quote the ancients in their very words, he not infrequently applies to painting passages which in their original connection had no bearing whatever on the subject. When, for instance, Winkelmann would tell us that the highest effect in art, as in poetry, cannot be attained by the mere imitation of nature, and that poet as well as painter should choose an impossibility which carries probability with it rather than what is simply possible, he adds: "This is perfectly consistent with Longinus' requirement of possibility and truth from the painter in opposition to the incredibility which he requires from the poet." Yet the addition was unfortunate, for it shows a seeming contradiction between the two great art critics which really does not exist. Longinus never said what is here attributed to him. Something similar he does say with regard to eloquence and poetry, but by no means of poetry and painting. *Ὡς δ' ἕτερόν τι ἡ ῥητορικὴ φαντασία βούλεται, καὶ ἕτερον ἡ παρὰ ποιηταῖς, οὐκ ἂν λάθοι σε, οὐδ' ὅτι τῆς μὲν ἐν ποιήσει τέλος ἐστὶν ἔκπληξις, τῆς δ' ἐν λόγοις ἐνάργεια*, he writes to his friend Terentian;[1] and again, *Ὀυ μὴν ἀλλὰ τὰ μὲν παρὰ τοῖς ποιηταῖς μυθικωτέραν ἔχει τὴν ὑπερέκπτωσιν, καὶ παντῇ τὸ πιστὸν ὑπεραίρουσαν· τῆς δὲ ῥητορικῆς φαντασίας, κάλλιστον ἀεὶ ἔμπρακτον καὶ ἐναληθές.*[2]

But Junius interpolates here painting instead of oratory, and it was in his writings, not in those of Longinus, that Winkelmann read: "Præsertim cum poeticæ phantasiæ finis sit *ἔκπληξις*, pictoriæ vero, *ἐνάργεια, καὶ τὰ μὲν παρὰ τοῖς ποιηταῖς*, ut loquitur idem

[1] Περὶ Ὕψους, τμῆμα, ιδ' (edit. T. Fabri), p. 36, 39. "But so it is that rhetorical figures aim at one thing, poetical figures at quite another; since in poetry emphasis is the main object, in rhetoric distinctness."

[2] "So with the poets, legends and exaggeration obtain and in all transcend belief; but in rhetorical figures the best is always the practicable and the true.

Longinus," &c.[1] The words of Longinus, to be sure, but not his meaning.

The same must have been the case with the following remark:[2] "All motions and attitudes of Greek figures which were too wild and fiery to be in accordance with the character of wisdom, were accounted as faults by the old masters and classed by them under the general name of *parenthyrsus*." The old masters? There can be no authority for that except Junius. *Parenthyrsus* was a word used in rhetoric, and, as a passage in Longinus would seem to show, even there peculiar to Theodorus.[3] *Τούτῳ παράκειται τρίτον τι κακίας εἶδος ἐν τοῖς παθητικοῖς, ὅπερ ὁ Θεόδωρος παρένθυρσον ἐκάλει· ἔστι δὲ πάθος ἄκαιρον καὶ κενόν, ἔνθα μὴ δεῖ πάθους· ἢ ἄμετρον, ἔνθα μετρίου δεῖ.*

I doubt, indeed, whether this word can be translated into the language of painting. For in oratory and poetry pathos can be carried to extreme without becoming *parenthyrsus*, which is only the extreme of pathos in the wrong place. But in painting the extreme of pathos would always be *parenthyrsus*, whatever its excuse in the circumstances of the persons concerned.

So, also, various errors in the "History of Art" have arisen solely from Winkelmann's haste in accept-

[1] De Pictura Vet. lib. i. cap. 4, p. 33.

[2] Von der Nachahmung der griech. Werke, &c., 23.

[3] Τμῆμα, β. "Next to this is a third form of faultiness in pathos, which Theodorus calls *parenthyrsus*; it is a pathos unseasonable and empty, where pathos is not necessary; or immoderate, where it should be moderate."

ing Junius instead of consulting the original authors. When, for instance, he is citing examples to show that excellence in all departments of art and labor was so highly prized by the Greeks, that the best workman, even on an insignificant thing, might immortalize his name, he brings forward this among others:[1] "We know the name of a maker of very exact balances or scales; he was called Parthenius." Winkelmann must have read the words of Juvenal, "lances Parthenio factas," which he here appeals to, only in Junius's catalogue. Had he looked up the original passage in Juvenal, he would not have been misled by the double meaning of the word "lanx," but would at once have seen from the connection that the poet was not speaking of balances or scales, but of plates and dishes. Juvenal is praising Catullus for throwing overboard his treasures during a violent storm at sea, in order to save the ship and himself. In his description of these treasures, he says: —

> Ille nec argentum dubitabat mittere, lances
> Parthenio factas, urnæ cratera capacem
> Et dignum sitiente Pholo, vel conjuge Fusci.
> Adde et bascaudas et mille escaria, multum
> Cælati, biberet quo callidus emtor Olynthi.

What can the "lances" be which are here standing among drinking-cups and bowls, but plates and dishes? And what does Juvenal mean, except that Catullus threw overboard his whole silver table-service, including plates made by Parthenius. "Par-

[1] Geschichte der Kunst, part i. p. 136.

thenius," says the old scholiast, "cœlatoris nomen" (the name of the engraver). But when Grangäus, in his annotations, appends to this name, "sculptor, de quo Plinius" (sculptor spoken of by Pliny), he must have been writing at random, for Pliny speaks of no artist of that name.

"Yes," continues Winkelmann, "even the name of the saddler, as we should call him, has been preserved, who made the leather shield of Ajax." This he cannot have derived from the source to which he refers his readers, — the life of Homer, by Herodotus. Here, indeed, the lines from the Iliad are quoted wherein the poet applies to this worker in leather the name Tychius. But it is at the same time expressly stated that this was the name of a worker in leather of Homer's acquaintance, whose name he thus introduced in token of his friendship and gratitude.[1]

Ἀπέδωκε δὲ χάριν καὶ Τυχίῳ τῷ σκύτει. ὃς ἐδέξατο αὐτὸν ἐν τῷ Νέῳ τείχει, προσελθόντα πρὸς τὸ σκύτειον, ἐν τοὶς ἔπεσι καταζεῦξας ἐν τῇ Ἰλιάδι τοῖς δε:

> *Αἴας δ' ἐγγύθεν ἦλθε, φέρων σάκος ἠύτε πύργον,*
> *χάλκεον, ἑπταβόειον· ὅ οἱ Τύχιος κάμε τεύχων*
> *σκυτοτόμων ὄχ' ἄριστος, Ὕλῃ ἔνι οἴκια ναίων·*[2]

Here we have exactly the opposite of what Winkelmann asserts. So utterly forgotten, even in Homer's time, was the name of the saddler who made the

[1] Herodotus de Vita Homeri, p. 756 (edit. Wessel).
[2] Iliad, vii.

shield of Ajax, that the poet was at liberty to substitute that of a perfect stranger.

Various other little errors I have found which are mere slips of memory, or concern things introduced merely as incidental illustrations.

For instance, it was Hercules, not Bacchus, who, as Parrhasius boasts, appeared to him in the same shape he had given him on the canvas.[1]

Tauriscus was not from Rhodes, but from Tralles, in Lydia.[2]

The Antigone was not the first tragedy of Sophocles.[3]

But I refrain from multiplying such trifles.

Censoriousness it could not be taken for; but to those who know my great respect for Winkelmann it might seem trifling.

[1] Geschichte der Kunst, part i. p. 176. Plinius, lib. xxxv. sect. 36. Athenæus, lib. xii. p. 543.

[2] Geschichte der Kunst, part ii. p. 353. Plinius, lib. xxxvi. sect. 4.

[3] See Appendix, note 57.

NOTES TO THE LAOCOON.

NOTES TO THE LAOCOON.

NOTE 1, p. 8.

ANTIOCHUS (Anthol. lib. ii. cap. 4). Hardouin, in his commentary on Pliny (lib. xxxv. sect. 36), attributes this epigram to a certain Piso. But among all the Greek epigrammatists there is none of this name.

NOTE 2, p. 9.

FOR this reason Aristotle commanded that his pictures should not be shown to young persons, in order that their imagination might be kept as free as possible from all disagreeable images. (Polit. lib. viii. cap. 5, p. 526, edit. Conring.) Boden, indeed, would read Pausanias in this passage instead of Pauson, because that artist is known to have painted lewd figures (de Umbra poetica comment. 1, p. xiii). As if we needed a philosophic law-giver to teach us the necessity of keeping from youth such incentives to wantonness! A comparison of this with the well-known passage in the "Art of Poesy" would have led him to withhold his conjecture. There are commentators, as Kühn on Ælian (Var. Hist. lib. iv. cap. 3), who suppose the difference mentioned by Aristotle as existing between Polygnotus, Dionysius, and Pauson to consist in this: that Polygnotus painted gods and heroes; Dionysius, men; and Pauson, animals. They all painted human figures; and the fact that Pauson once painted a horse, does not prove him to have been a painter of animals as Boden supposes him to have been. Their rank was determined by the degree of beauty they gave their human figures;

and the reason that Dionysius could paint nothing but men, and was therefore called pre-eminently the anthropographist, was that he copied too slavishly, and could not rise into the domain of the ideal beneath which it would have been blasphemy to represent gods and heroes.

NOTE 3, p. 11.

THE serpent has been erroneously regarded as the peculiar symbol of a god of medicine. But Justin Martyr expressly says (Apolog. ii. p. 55, edit. Sylburgh), *παρὰ παντὶ τῶν νομιζομένων παρ' ὑμῖν θεῶν, ὄφις σύμβολον μέγα καὶ μυστήριον ἀναγράφεται*; and a number of monuments might be mentioned where the serpent accompanies deities having no connection with health.

NOTE 4, p. 12.

LOOK through all the works of art mentioned by Pliny, Pausanias, and the rest, examine all the remaining statues, bas-reliefs, and pictures of the ancients, and nowhere will you find a fury. I except figures that are rather symbolical than belonging to art, such as those generally represented on coins. Yet Spence, since he insisted on having furies, would have done better to borrow them from coins than introduce them by an ingenious conceit into a work where they certainly do not exist. (Seguini Numis. p. 178. Spanheim. de Præst. Numism. Dissert. xiii. p. 639. Les Césars de Julien, par Spanheim, p. 48. In his Polymetis he says (dial. xvi.): "Though furies are very uncommon in the works of the ancient artists, yet there is one subject in which they are generally introduced by them. I mean the death of Meleager, in the relievos of which they are often represented as encouraging or urging Althæa to burn the fatal brand on which the life of her only son depended. Even a woman's resentment, you see, could not go so far without a little help from the devil. In a copy of one of these relievos, published in the 'Admiranda,' there are two women standing by the altar with Althæa, who are probably meant for furies in the original, (for who but furies would assist at such a sacrifice?) though the copy scarce represents them horrid enough for that character. But what is most to be observed in that piece is the round disc beneath the centre of it, with the evident head of a fury upon it. This might be what Althæa addressed her prayers to whenever she wished ill to her neighbors, or whenever she was going to do any very evil action. Ovid introduces her as invoking the furies on this occasion in particular, and makes her give more than one reason for her doing so." (Metamorph. viii. 479.)

In this way we might make every thing out of any thing. "Who but furies," asks Spence, "would have assisted at such a sacrifice?" I answer, the maid-servants of Althæa, who had to kindle and feed the fire. Ovid says (Metamorph. viii.): —

> Protulit hunc (stipitem) genetrix, tædasque in fragmina poni
> Imperat, et positis inimicos admovet ignes.

"The mother brought the brand and commands torches to be placed upon the pieces, and applies hostile flame to the pile."

Both figures have actually in their hands these "tædas," long pieces of pine, such as the ancients used for torches, and one, as her attitude shows, has just broken such a piece. As little do I recognize a fury upon the disc towards the middle of the work. It is a face expressive of violent pain, — doubtless the head of Meleager himself (Metamorph. viii. 515).

> Inscius atque absens flamma Meleagros in illa
> Uritur; et cæcis torreri viscera sentit
> Ignibus; et magnos superat virtute dolores.

"Meleager, absent and unconscious, is consumed in that fire, and feels his bowels parched with the unseen flames; yet with courage he subdues the dreadful pains."

The artist used this as an introduction to the next incident of the same story, — the death of Meleager. What Spence makes furies, Montfaucon took to be fates, with the exception of the head upon the disc, which he also calls a fury. Bellori leaves it undecided whether they are fates or furies. An "or" which sufficiently proves that they are neither the one nor the other. Montfaucon's further interpretation should have been clearer. The female figure resting on her elbows by the bed, he should have called Cassandra, not Atalanta. Atalanta is the one sitting in a grieving attitude with her back towards the bed. The artist has very wisely turned her away from the family, as being only the beloved, not the wife, of Meleager, and because her distress at a calamity of which she had been the innocent cause must have exasperated his family.

NOTE 5, p. 14.

HE thus describes the degrees of sadness actually expressed by Timanthes: "Calchantem tristem, mæstum Ulyssem, clamantem Ajacem, lamentantem Menelaum." Ajax screaming would have been extremely ugly, and since neither Cicero nor Quintilian, when speaking of this picture, so describe him, I shall venture with the less hesitation to consider this an addition with which Valerius has enriched the canvas from his own invention.

NOTE 6, p. 15.

WE read in Pliny (lib. 34, sect. 19): "Eundem [Myro] vicit et Pythagoras Leontinus, qui fecit statiodromon Astylon, qui Olympiæ ostenditur: et Libyn puerum tenentem tabulam, eodem loco, et mala ferentem nudum. Syracusis autem claudicantem: cujus hulceris dolorem sentire etiam spectantes videntur." "Pythagoras Leontinus surpassed him (Myro). He made the statue of the runner, Astylon, which is exhibited at Olympia, and in the same place a Libyan boy holding a tablet, and a rude statue bearing apples; but at Syracuse a limping figure, the pain of whose sore the beholders themselves seem to feel." Let us examine these last words more closely. Is there not evident reference here to some person well known as having a painful ulcer? "Cujus hulceris," &c. And shall that "cujus" be made to refer simply to the "claudicantem," and the "claudicantem," perhaps, to the still more remote "puerum?" No one had more reason to be known by such a malady than Philoctetes. I read, therefore, for "claudicantem," "Philoctetem," or, at least, both together, "Philoctetem claudicantem," supposing that, as the words were so similar in sound, one had crowded out the other. Sophocles represents him as *στίβον κατ' ἀνάγκην ἕρπειν*, compelled to drag his limping gait, and his not being able to tread as firmly on his wounded foot would have occasioned a limp.

NOTE 7, p. 24.

WHEN the chorus perceives Philoctetes under this accumulation of miseries, his helpless solitude seems the circumstance that chiefly touches them. We hear in every word the social Greek. With regard to one passage, however, I have my doubts. It is this : —

> *Ἰν' αὐτὸς ἦν πρόσουρος οὐκ ἔχων βάσιν,*
> *οὐδέ τιν' ἐγχώρων,*
> *κακογέιτονα παρ' ᾧ στόνον ἀντίτυπον*
> *βαρυβρῶτ' ἀποκλαύ —*
> *σειεν αἱματηρόν.*

Lit. : I myself, my only neighbor, having no power to walk, nor any companion, a neighbor in ill, to whom I might wail forth my echoing, gnawing groans, bloodstained.

The common translation of Winshem renders the lines thus : —

> Ventis expositus et pedibus captus
> Nullum cohabitatorem
> Nec vicinum ullum saltem malum habens, apud quem gemitum mutuum.
> Gravemque ac cruentum
> Ederet.

The translation of Thomas Johnson differs from this only in the choice of words : —

> Ubi ipse ventis erat expositus, firmum gradum non habens,
> Nec quenquam indigenarum,
> Nec malum vicinum, apud quem ploraret
> Vehementur edacem
> Sanguineum morbum, mutuo gemitu.

One might think he had borrowed these words from the translation of Thomas Naogeorgus, who expresses himself thus (his work is very rare, and Fabricius himself knew it only through Operin's Catalogue): —

> . . . ubi expositus fuit
> Ventis ipse, gradum firmum haud habens,
> Nec quenquam indigenam, nec vel malum
> Vicinum, ploraret apud quem
> Vehementer edacem atque cruentum
> Morbum mutuo.

If these translations are correct, the chorus pronounces the strongest possible eulogy on human society. The wretch has no human being near him; he knows of no friendly neighbor; even a bad one would have been happiness. Thomson, then, might have had this passage in mind when he puts these words into the mouth of his Melisander, who was likewise abandoned by ruffians on a desert island: —

> Cast on the wildest of the Cyclad isles
> Where never human foot had marked the shore,
> These ruffians left me; yet believe me, Arcas,
> Such is the rooted love we bear mankind,
> All ruffians as they were, I never heard
> A sound so dismal as their parting oars.

To him, also, the society of ruffians was better than none. A great and admirable idea! If we could but be sure that Sophocles, too, had meant to express it! But I must reluctantly confess to finding nothing of the sort in him, unless, indeed, I were to use, instead of my own eyes, those of the old scholiast, who thus transposes the words: — *Οὐ μόνον ὅπου καλὸν οὐκ εἶχέ τινα τῶν ἐγχωρίων γείτονα, ἀλλὰ οὐδὲ κακόν, παρ' οὗ ἀμοιβαῖον λόγον στενάζων ἀκούσειε.* Brumoy, as well as our modern German translator, has held to this reading, like the translators quoted above. Brumoy says, "Sans société, même importune;" and the German, "jeder Gesellschaft, auch der beschwerlichsten, beraubt." My reasons for differing from all of these are the following. First, it is evident that if *κακογείτονα* was meant to be separated from *τιν' ἐγχώρων* and constitute a distinct clause, the particle *οὐδέ* would necessarily have been repeated before it. Since this is not the case, it is equally evident that *κακογείτονα* belongs to *τίνα*, and there should be no comma after *ἐγχώρων*. This comma crept in from the translation. Accordingly, I find that some Greek editions (as that published at Wittenberg of 1585 in 8vo, which was wholly unknown to Fabricius) are without it, but put a comma only after *κακογείτονα*, as is proper. Secondly, is that a bad neighbor from whom we may expect, as the scholiast has it, *στόνον ἀντίτυπον, ἀμοιβαῖον*? To mingle his sighs with ours is the office of a friend, not an enemy. In short, the word *κακογείτονα* has not been rightly understood. It has been thought to be derived from the adjective *κακός*, when it is really derived from the substantive *τὸ κακόν*. It has been translated an evil neighbor, instead of a neighbor in ill. Just as *κακόμαντις* means not an evil, in the sense of a false, untrue prophet, but a prophet of evil, and *κακότεχνος* means not a bad, unskilful painter, but a painter of bad things. In this passage the poet means by a neighbor in ill, one who is overtaken by a similar misfortune with ourselves, or from friendship shares our sufferings; so that the whole expression, *οὐδ' ἔχων τιν' ἐγχώρων κακογείτονα*, is to be translated simply by "neque quenquam indigenarum mali socium habens." The new English translator of Sophocles, Thomas Franklin, must have been of my opinion. Neither does he find an evil neighbor in *κακογείτων*, but translates it simply "fellow-mourner."

> Exposed to the inclement skies,
> Deserted and forlorn he lies,
> No friend nor fellow-mourner there,
> To soothe his sorrow and divide his care.

NOTE 8, p. 34.

SATURNAL. lib. v. cap. 2. "Non parva sunt alia quæ Virgilius traxit a Græcis, dicturumne me putatis quæ vulgo nota sunt? quod Theocritum sibi fecerit pastoralis operis autorem, ruralis Hesiodum? et quod in ipsis Georgicis, tempestatis serenitatisque signa de Arati Phænomenis traxerit? vel quod eversionem Trojæ, cum Sinone suo, et equo ligneo cæterisque omnibus, quæ librum secundum faciunt, a Pisandro pene ad verbum transcripserit? qui inter Græcos poetas eminet opere, quod a nuptiis Jovis et Junonis incipiens universas historias, quæ mediis omnibus sæculis usque ad ætatem ipsius Pisandri contigerunt, in unam seriem coactas redegerit, et unum ex diversis hiatibus temporum corpus effecerit? in quo opere inter historias cæteras interitus quoque Trojæ in hunc modum relatus est. Quæ fideliter Maro interpretando, fabricatus est sibi Iliacæ urbis ruinam. Sed et hæc et talia ut pueris decantata prætereo."

Not a few other things were brought by Virgil from the Greeks, and inserted in his poem as original. Do you think I would speak of what is known to all the world? how he took his pastoral poem from Theocritus, his rural from Hesiod? and how, in his Georgics, he took from the Phenomena of Aratus the signs of winter and summer? or that he translated almost word for word from Pisander the destruction of Troy, with his Sinon and wooden horse and the rest? For he is famous among Greek poets for a work in which, beginning his universal history with the nuptials of Jupiter and Juno, he collected into one series whatever had happened in all ages, to the time of himself, Pisander. In which work the destruction of Troy, among other things, is related in the same way. By faithfully interpreting these things, Maro made his ruin of Ilium. But these, and others like them, I pass over as familiar to every schoolboy.

NOTE 9, p. 35.

I DO not forget that a picture mentioned by Eumolpus in Petronius may be cited in contradiction of this. It represented the destruction of Troy, and particularly the history of Laocoon exactly as narrated by Virgil. And since, in the same gallery at Naples were other old pictures by Zeuxis, Protogenes, and Apelles, it was inferred that this was also an old Greek picture. But permit me to say that a novelist is no historian. This gallery and picture, and Eumolpus himself, apparently existed only in the imagination of Petronius. That the whole was fiction appears from the evident traces of an almost schoolboyish imitation of Virgil. Thus Virgil (Æneid lib. ii. 199–224) : —

Hic aliud majus miseris multoque tremendum
Objicitur magis, atque improvida pectora turbat.
Laocoon, ductus Neptuno sorte sacerdos,
Solemnis taurum ingentem mactabat ad aras.
Ecce autem gemini a Tenedo tranquilla per alta
(Horresco referens) immensis orbibus angues
Incumbunt pelago, pariterque ad litora tendunt:
Pectora quorum inter fluctus arrecta, jubæque
Sanguineæ exsuperant undas: pars cetera pontum
Pone legit, sinuatque immensa volumine terga.
Fit sonitus, spumante salo: jamque arva tenebant,
Ardentesque oculos suffecti sanguine et igni
Sibila lambebant linguis vibrantibus ora.
Diffugimus visu exsangues. Illi agmine certo
Laocoonta petunt, et primum parva duorum
Corpora natorum serpens amplexus uterque
Implicat, et miseros morsu depascitur artus.
Post ipsum, auxilio subeuntem ac tela ferentem,
Corripiunt, spirisque ligant ingentibus; et jam
Bis medium amplexi, bis collo squamea circum
Terga dati, superant capite et cervicibus altis.
Ille simul manibus tendit divellere nodos,
Perfusus sanie vittas atroque veneno:
Clamores simul horrendos ad sidera tollit.
Quales mugitus, fugit cum saucius aram
Taurus et incertam excussit cervice securim.

And thus Eumolpus, in whose lines, as is usually the case with improvisators, memory has had as large a share as imagination:—

Ecce alia monstra. Celsa qua Tenedos mare
Dorso repellit, tumida consurgunt freta,
Undaque resultat scissa tranquillo minor.
Qualis silenti nocte remorum sonus
Longe refertur, cum premunt classes mare,
Pulsumque marmor abiete imposita gemit.
Respicimus, angues orbibus geminis ferunt
Ad saxa fluctus: tumida quorum pectora
Rates ut altæ, lateribus spumas agunt:
Dat cauda sonitum; liberæ ponto jubæ
Coruscant luminibus, fulmineum jubar

Incendit æquor, sibilisque undæ tremunt:
Stupuere mentes. Infulis stabant sacri
Phrygioque cultu gemina nati pignora
Laocoonte, quos repente tergoribus ligant
Angues corusci: parvulas illi manus
Ad ora referunt: neuter auxilio sibi
Uterque fratri transtulit pias vices,
Morsque ipsa miseros mutuo perdit metu.
Accumulat ecce liberûm funus parens
Infirmus auxiliator; invadunt virum
Jam morte pasti, membraque ad terram trahunt.
Jacet sacerdos inter aras victima.

The main points are the same in both, and in many places the same words are used. But those are trifles, and too evident to require mention. There are other signs of imitation, more subtle, but not less sure. If the imitator be a man with confidence in his own powers, he seldom imitates without trying to improve upon the original; and, if he fancy himself to have succeeded, he is enough of a fox to brush over with his tail the footprints which might betray his course. But he betrays himself by this very vanity of wishing to introduce embellishments, and his desire to appear original. For his embellishments are nothing but exaggerations and excessive refinements. Virgil says, "Sanguineæ jubæ"; Petronius, "liberæ jubæ luminibus coruscant"; Virgil, "ardentes oculos suffecti sanguine et igni"; Petronius, "fulmineum jubar incendit æquor." Virgil, "fit sonitus spumante salo"; Petronius, "sibilis undæ tremunt." So the imitator goes on exaggerating greatness into monstrosity, wonders into impossibilities. The boys are secondary in Virgil. He passes them over with a few insignificant words, indicative simply of their helplessness and distress. Petronius makes a great point of them, converting the two children into a couple of heroes.

Neuter auxilio sibi
Uterque fratri transtulit pias vices
Morsque ipsa miseros mutuo perdit metu.

Who expects from human beings, and children especially, such self-sacrifice? The Greek understood nature better (Quintus

Calaber, lib. xii.), when he made even mothers forget their children at the appearance of the terrible serpents, so intent was every one on securing his own safety.

> . . . ἐνθα γυναῖκες
> Οἰμωζον, καὶ πού τις ἑῶν ἐπελήσατο τέκνων
> Αὐτῇ ἀλευομένη στυγερὸν μόρον . . .

The usual method of trying to conceal an imitation is to alter the shading, bringing forward what was in shadow, and obscuring what was in relief. Virgil lays great stress upon the size of the serpents, because the probability of the whole subsequent scene depends upon it. The noise occasioned by their coming is a secondary idea, intended to make more vivid the impression of their size. Petronius raises this secondary idea into chief prominence, describing the noise with all possible wealth of diction, and so far forgetting to describe the size of the monsters that we are almost left to infer it from the noise they make. He hardly would have fallen into this error, had he been drawing solely from his imagination, with no model before him which he wished to imitate without the appearance of imitation. We can always recognize a poetic picture as an unsuccessful imitation when we find minor details exaggerated and important ones neglected, however many incidental beauties the poem may possess, and however difficult, or even impossible, it may be to discover the original.

Note 10, p. 36.

Suppl. aux Antiq. Expl. T. i. p. 243. Il y a quelque petite différence entre ce que dit Virgile, et ce que le marbre représente. Il semble, selon ce que dit le poëte, que les serpens quittèrent les deux enfans pour venir entortiller le père, au lieu que dans ce marbre ils lient en même temps les enfans et leur père.

Note 11, p. 37.

Donatus ad v. 227, lib. ii. Æneid. Mirandum non est, clypeo et simulacri vestigiis tegi potuisse, quos supra et longos et validos dixit, et multiplici ambitu circumdedisse Laocoontis corpus ac liberorum, et fuisse superfluam partem. The "non" in the clause "mirandum non est," should, it seems to me, be omitted, unless we suppose the concluding part of the sentence to be missing. For, since the serpents were of such extraordinary length, it would certainly be surprising that they could be concealed beneath the goddess's shield, unless this also were of great length, and belonged to a colossal figure. The assurance that this was actually the case must have been meant to follow, or the "non" has no meaning.

NOTE 12, p. 39.

IN the handsome edition of Dryden's Virgil (London, 1697). Yet here the serpents are wound but once about the body, and hardly at all about the neck. So indifferent an artist scarcely deserves an excuse, but the only one that could be made for him would be that prints are merely illustrations, and by no means to be regarded as independent works of art.

NOTE 13, p. 40.

THIS is the judgment of De Piles in his remarks upon Du Fresnoy: "Remarquez, s'il vous plaît, que les draperies tendres et légères, n'étant données qu'au sexe féminin, les anciens sculpteurs ont évité autant qu'ils ont pu, d'habiller les figures d'hommes; parce qu'ils ont pensé, comme nous l'avons déjà dit qu'en sculpture on ne pouvait imiter les étoffes, et que les gros plis faisaient un mauvais effet. Il y a presque autant d'exemples de cette vérité, qu'il y a parmi les antiques, de figures d'hommes nuds. Je rapporterai seulement celui du Laocoon, lequel, selon la vraisemblance, devrait être vêtu. En effet, quelle apparence y a-t-il qu'un fils de roi, qu'un prêtre d'Apollon, se trouvât tout nud dans la cérémonie actuelle d'un sacrifice? car les serpens passèrent de l'île de Tenedos au rivage de Troye, et surprirent Laocoon et ses fils dans le temps même qu'il sacrifiait à Neptune sur le bord de la mer, comme le marque Virgile dans le second livre de son Enéide. Cependant les artistes qui sont les auteurs de ce bel ouvrage, ont bien vu qu'ils ne pouvaient pas leur donner de vêtements convenables à leur qualité, sans faire comme un amas de pierres, dont la masse ressemblerait à un rocher, au lieu des trois admirables figures, qui ont été, et qui sont toujours, l'admiration des siècles. C'est pour cela que de deux inconveniens, ils ont jugé celui des draperies beaucoup plus fâcheux, que celui d'aller contre la vérité même.

NOTE 14, p. 42.

MAFFEI, Richardson, and, more recently, Herr Von Hagedorn. (Betrachtungen über die Malerei, p. 37. Richardson, Traité de la Peinture, vol. iii.) De Fontaines does not merit being reckoned in the same class with these scholars. In the notes to his translation of Virgil, he maintains, indeed, that the poet had the group in mind, but he is so ignorant as to ascribe it to Phidias.

NOTE 15, p. 44.

I CAN adduce no better argument in support of my view than this poem of Sadolet. It is worthy of one of the old poets, and, since it may well take the place of an engraving, I venture to introduce it here entire.

DE LAOCOONTIS STATUA JACOBI SADOLETI CARMEN.

Ecce alto terræ e cumulo, ingentisque ruinæ
Visceribus, iterum reducem longinqua reduxit
Laocoonta dies; aulis regalibus olim
Qui stetit, atque tuos ornabat, Tite, Penates.
Divinæ simulacrum artis, nec docta vetustas
Nobilius spectabat opus, nunc celsa revisit
Exemptum tenebris redivivæ mœnia Romæ.
Quid primum summumque loquar? miserumne parentem
Et prolem geminam? an sinuatos flexibus angues
Terribili aspectu? caudasque irasque draconum
Vulneraque et veros, saxo moriente, dolores?
Horret ad hæc animus, mutaque ab imagine pulsat
Pectora, non parvo pietas commixta tremori.
Prolixum bini spiris glomerantur in orbem
Ardentes colubri, et sinuosis orbibus errant,

Ternaque multiplici constringunt corpora nexu.
Vix oculi sufferre valent, crudele tuendo
Exitium, casusque feros: micat alter, et ipsum
Laocoonta petit, totumque infraque supraque
Implicat et rabido tandem ferit ilia morsu.
Connexum refugit corpus, torquentia sese
Membra, latusque retro sinuatum a vulnere cernas.
Ille dolore acri, et laniatu impulsus acerbo,
Dat gemitum ingentem, crudosque evellere dentes
Connixus, lævam impatiens ad terga Chelydri
Objicit: intendunt nervi, collectaque ab omni
Corpore vis frustra summis conatibus instat.
Ferre nequit rabiem, et de vulnere murmur anhelum est.
At serpens lapsu crebro redeunte subintrat
Lubricus, intortoque ligat genua infima nodo.
Absistunt suræ, spirisque prementibus arctum
Crus tumet, obsepto turgent vitalia pulsu,
Liventesque atro distendunt sanguine venas.
Nec minus in natos eadem vis effera sævit
Implexuque angit rapido, miserandaque membra
Dilacerat: jamque alterius depasta cruentum
Pectus, suprema genitorem voce cientis,
Circumjectu orbis, validoque volumine fulcit.
Alter adhuc nullo violatus corpora morsu,
Dum parat adducta caudam divellere planta,
Horret ad aspectum miseri patris, hæret in illo,
Et jam jam ingentes fletus, lachrymasque cadentes
Anceps in dubio retinet timor. Ergo perenni
Qui tantum statuistis opus jam laude nitentes,
Artifices magni (quanquam et melioribus actis
Quæritur æternum nomen, multoque licebat
Clarius ingenium venturæ tradere famæ)
Attamen ad laudem quæcunque oblata facultas
Egregium hanc rapere, et summa ad fastigia niti.
Vos rigidum lapidem vivis animare figuris
Eximii, et vivos spiranti in marmore sensus
Inserere, aspicimus motumque iramque doloremque,
Et pene audimus gemitus; vos extulit olim
Clara Rhodos, vestræ jacuerunt artis honores
Tempore ab immenso, quos rursum in luce secunda
Roma videt, celebratque frequens: operisque vetusti
Gratia parta recens. Quanto præstantius ergo est
Ingenio, aut quovis extendere fata labore,
Quam fastus et opes et inanem extendere luxum.

LAOCOON, BY JAMES SADOLET.

So, from the depths of earth and the bowels of mighty ruins, the long-deferred day has brought back the returning Laocoon, who stood of old in thy royal halls and graced thy penates, Titus. The image of divine art, a work as noble as any produced by the learning of antiquity, now freed from darkness, beholds again the lofty walls of renovated Rome. With what part shall I begin as the greatest? the unhappy father and his two sons? the sinuous coils of the terrible serpents? the tails and the fierceness of the dragons? the wounds and real pains of the dying stone? These chill the mind with horror, and pity, mingled with no slight fear, drives our hearts back from the dumb image. Two gleaming snakes cover a vast space with their gathered coils, and move in sinuous rings, and hold three bodies bound in a many-twisted knot. Eyes scarce can bear to behold the cruel death and fierce sufferings. One gleaming seeks Laocoon himself, winding him all about, above, below, and attacks his groins at last with poisonous bite. The imprisoned body recoils, and you see the limbs writhe and the side shrink back from the wound. Forced by the sharp pain and bitter anguish, he groans; and, trying to tear out the cruel teeth, throws his left hand upon the serpent's back. The nerves strain, and the whole body in vain collects its strength for the supreme effort. He cannot endure the fierce torture, and pants from the wound. But the slippery snake glides down with frequent folds, and binds his leg below the knee with twisted knot. The calves fall in, the tight-bound leg swells between the pressing coils, and the vitals grow tumid from the stopping of the pulses, and black blood distends the livid veins. The same cruel violence attacks the children no less fiercely, tortures them with many encircling folds, and lacerates their suffering limbs. Now satiated upon the bloody breast of one, who, with his last breath, calls upon his father, the serpent supports the lifeless body with the mighty circles thrown around it. The other, whose body has as yet been hurt by no sting, while preparing to pluck out the tail from his foot, is filled with horror at sight of his wretched father, and clings to him. A double fear restrains his great sobs and falling tears. Therefore ye enjoy perpetual fame, ye great artificers who made the mighty work, although an immortal name may be sought by better deeds, and nobler talents may be handed down to future fame. Yet any power employed to snatch this praise and reach the heights of fame is excellent. Ye have excelled in animating the rigid stone with living forms, and inserting living senses within the breathing marble. We see the movement, the wrath and pain, and almost hear the groans. Illustrious Rhodes begot you of old. Long the glories of your art lay hid, but Rome beholds them again in a second dawn, and celebrates them with many voices, in fresh acknowledgment of the old labor. How much nobler, then, to extend our fates by art or toil than to swell pride and wealth and empty luxury.

(Leodegarii a Quercu Farrago Poematum, T. ii.) Gruter has

introduced this poem with another one of Sadolet into his well-known collection, but with many errors. (Delic. Poet. Italorum. Parte alt.)

NOTE 16, p. 45.

DE la Peinture, tome iii. p. 516. C'est l'horreur que les Troïens ont conçue contre Laocoon, qui était nécessaire à Virgile pour la conduite de son poëme; et cela le mène à cette description pathétique de la destruction de la patrie de son héros. Aussi Virgile n'avait garde de diviser l'attention sur la dernière nuit, pour une grand ville entière, par la peinture d'un petit malheur d'un particulier.

NOTE 17, p. 51.

I SAY it is possible, but I would wager ten against one that it is not so. Juvenal is speaking of the early days of the republic, when splendor and luxury were yet unknown, and the soldier put whatever gold and silver he got as booty upon his arms and the caparisons of his horse. (Sat. xi.)

Tunc rudis et Grajas mirari nescius artes
Urbibus eversis prædarum in parte reperta
Magnorum artificum frangebat pocula miles.
Ut phaleris gauderet equus, cælataque cassis
Romuleæ simulacra feræ mansuescere jussæ
Imperii fato, geminos sub rupe Quirinos,
Ac nudam effigiem clypeo fulgentis et hasta,
Pendentisque Dei perituro ostenderet hosti.

The soldier broke up the precious cups, the masterpieces of great artists, to make a she-wolf, a little Romulus and Remus to deck his helmet with. All is plain down to the last two lines, where the poet proceeds to describe such a figure on the helmets of the old soldiers. The figure is meant for the god Mars, but what can the term *pendentis* mean as applied to him? Rigaltius found in an old gloss the interpretation "quasi ad ictum se inclinantis." Lubinus supposes the figure to have been on the shield, and, as the shield hung from the arm, the figure might be spoken of as hanging. But this is contrary to the construction, the subject of "ostenderet" being not "miles" but "cassis." According to Britannicus, whatever stands high in the air may be said to hang, and the expression may be used of this figure perched above or upon the helmet. Some would read "perdentis" as a contrast to the following "perituro," though none but themselves would think the contrast desirable. What does Addison say to this doubtful passage? He thinks all the commentators are wrong and maintains this to be the true meaning. "The Roman soldiers, who were not a little proud of their founder and the military genius of their republic, used to bear on their helmets the first history of Romulus, who was begot by the god of war and suckled by a wolf. The figure of the god was made as if descending upon the priestess Ilia, or, as others call her, Rhea Silvia. As he was represented descending, his figure appeared suspended in the air over the vestal virgin, in which sense the word 'pendentis' is extremely proper and poetical. Besides the antique basso-rilievo (in Bellori) that made me first think of this interpretation, I have since met with the same figures on the reverses of a couple of ancient coins, which were stamped in the reign of Antoninus Pius." (Addison's Travels, Rome, Tonson's edition, 1745, p. 183.)

Since Spence considers this such a happy discovery on the part of Addison, that he quotes it as a model of its kind and as the strongest proof of the value of the works of the old artists in throwing light on the classic Roman poets, I cannot refrain from a closer examination of it. (Polymetis, dial. vii.) I must observe, in the first place, that the bas-relief and the coin would hardly have recalled to Addison the passage from Juvenal, had he not remembered reading in the old scholiast, who substituted "venientis" for "fulgentis" in the last line but one, this interpretation: "Martis ad illam venientis ut concumberet." Now, instead of this reading of the old scholiast, let us accept Addison's, and see if we have then the slightest reason for supposing the poet to have had Rhea in mind. Would it not rather be a complete inversion on his part, where he is speaking of the wolf and the boys, to be thinking of the adventure to which the children owe their life? Rhea has not yet become a mother, and the boys are already lying under the rock. Would an hour of dalliance be a fitting emblem for the helmet of a Roman soldier? The soldier was proud of the divine origin of the founder of his country, and that was sufficiently typified by the wolf and the children. What need of introducing Mars at a moment when he was any thing but the dread-inspiring god? His visit to Rhea may have been represented on any number of old marbles and coins: did that make it a fitting ornament for armor? What are the marbles and coins on which Addison saw Mars in this hovering attitude? The old bas-relief to which he appeals is said to be in Bellori, but we shall look for it in vain in the Admiranda, his collection of finest old bas-reliefs. Spence cannot have found it there or elsewhere, for he makes no mention of it. Nothing remains, therefore, but the coins, which we will study from Addison himself. I see a recumbent figure of Rhea, and Mars standing on a somewhat higher plane, because there was not room for him on the same level. That is all: there is no sign of his being suspended. Such an effect is produced very strongly, it is true, in Spence's copy. The upper part of the figure is thrown so far forward as to make standing impossible; so that if the body be not falling, it must be hovering. Spence says this coin is in his possession. It is hard to question a man's veracity, even in a trifle, but our eyes are often greatly influenced by a preconceived opinion. He may, besides, have thought it allowable for the good of the reader to have the artist so emphasize the expression which he thought he saw, that as little doubt might remain on our mind as on his. One thing is plain: that Spence and Addison refer to the same coin, which is either very much misrepresented by one or embellished by the other. But I have another objection to make to this supposed hovering attitude of Mars. A body thus suspended, without any visible cause for the law of gravitation not acting upon it, is an absurdity of which no example can be found in the old works of art. It is not allowable even in modern painting. If a body is to be suspended in the air, it must either have wings or appear to rest upon something, if only a cloud. When Homer makes Thetis rise on foot from the sea-shore to Olympus, Τὴν μὲν ἄρ' Οὔλυμπόνδε πόδες φέρον (Iliad, xviii. 148), Count Caylus is too well aware of the limitations of art to counsel the painter to represent her as walking unsupported through the air. She must pursue her way upon a cloud (Tableaux tirés de l'Iliade, p. 91), as in another place he puts her into a chariot (p. 131), although exactly the opposite is stated by the poet. How can it be otherwise? Although the poet represents the goddess with a human body, he yet removes from her every trace of coarse and heavy materiality, and animates her with a power which raises her beyond the influence of our laws of motion. How could painting so distinguish the bodily shape of a deity from the bodily shape of a human being, that our eyes should not be offended by observing it acted upon by different laws of motion, weight, and equilibrium? How but by conventional signs, such as a pair of wings or a cloud? But more of this elsewhere; here it is enough to require the defenders of the Addison theory to show on the old monuments a second figure floating thus unsupported in the air. Can this Mars be the only one of its kind? why? Were there some particular conditions handed down by tradition which would necessitate such exceptional treatment in this one case? There is no trace of such in Ovid (Fast. lib. i.), but rather proof that no such conditions ever could have existed. For in other ancient works of art which represent the same story, Mars is evidently not hovering, but walking. Examine the bas-relief in Montfaucon (Suppl. T. i. p. 183), which is to be found, if I am not mistaken, in the Mellini palace at Rome. Rhea lies asleep under a tree, and Mars approaches her softly, with that expressive backward motion of the right hand by which we warn those behind to stay where they are, or to advance gently. His attitude is precisely the same as on the coin, except that in one case he holds his lance in the right, in the other in the left hand. We often find famous statues and bas-reliefs copied on coins, and the same may well be the case here, only that the cutter of the die did not perceive the force of the backward motion of the hand, and thought it better employed in holding the lance. Taking all these arguments into consideration, what degree of probability remains to Addison's theory? Hardly more than a bare possibility. But where can better explanation be had if this fails? Possibly among the interpretations rejected by Addison. But if not, what then? The passage in the poet is corrupted, and so it must remain. It certainly will so remain, if twenty new conjectures are invented. We might say that "pendentis" here was to be taken figuratively in the sense of uncertain, undecided. Mars "pendens" would then be the same as Mars "incertus" or Mars "communis." "Dii communes," says Servius (ad. v. 118, lib. xii. Æneid), are Mars, Bellona, and Victory, so called from their favoring both parties in war. And the line, —

Pendentisque Dei (effigiem) perituro ostenderet hosti,

would mean that the old Roman soldier was accustomed to wear the image of the impartial god in the presence of his enemy, who, in spite of the impartiality, was soon to perish. A very subtle idea, making the victories of the old Romans depend more upon their own bravery than on the friendly aid of their founder. Nevertheless, "non liquet."

NOTE 18, p. 51.

"TILL I got acquainted with these Auræ (or sylphs)," says Spence (Polymetis, dial. xiii.), "I found myself always at a loss in reading the known story of Cephalus and Procris in Ovid. I could never imagine how Cephalus crying out, 'Aura venias' (though in ever so languishing a manner), could give anybody a suspicion of his being false to Procris. As I had been always used to think that Aura signified only the air in general, or a gentle breeze in particular, I thought Procris's jealousy less founded than the most extravagant jealousies generally are. But when I had once found that Aura might signify a very handsome young woman as well as the air, the case was entirely altered, and the story seemed to go on in a very reasonable manner." I will not take back in the note the approval bestowed in the text on this discovery, on which Spence so plumes himself. But I cannot refrain from remarking that, even without it, the passage was very natural and intelligible. We only needed to know that Aura occurs frequently among the ancients as a woman's name. According to Nonnus, for instance (Dionys. lib. xlviii.), the nymph of Diana was thus named, who, for claiming to possess a more manly beauty than the goddess herself, was, as a punishment for her presumption, exposed in her sleep to the embraces of Bacchus.

NOTE 19, p. 52.

JUVENALIS Satyr. viii. v. 52–55.

> . . . At tu
> Nil nisi Cecropides; truncoque simillimus Hermæ!
> Nullo quippe alio vincis discrimine, quam quod
> Illi marmoreum caput est, tua vivit imago.

"But thou art nothing if not a descendant of Cecrops; in body most like a Hermes; forsooth the only thing in which you surpass that, is that your head is a living image, while the Hermes is marble." If Spence had embraced the old Greek writers in his work, a fable of Æsop might perhaps — and yet perhaps not — have occurred to him, which throws still clearer light upon this passage in Juvenal. "Mercury," Æsop tells us, "wishing to know in what repute he stood among men, concealed his divinity, and entered a sculptor's studio. Here he beheld a statue of Jupiter, and asked its value. 'A drachm,' was the answer. Mercury smiled. 'And this Juno?' he asked again. 'About the same.' The god meanwhile had caught sight of his own image, and thought to himself, — 'I, as the messenger of the gods, from whom come all gains, must be much more highly prized by men.' 'And this god,' he asked, pointing to his own image, 'how dear might that be?' 'That?' replied the artist, 'buy the other two, and I will throw that in.'" Mercury went away sadly crestfallen. But the artist did not recognize him, and could therefore have had no intention of wounding his self-love. The reason for his set ting so small a value on the statue must have lain in its work manship. The less degree of reverence due to the god whom it represented could have had nothing to do with the matter, for the artist values his works according to the skill, industry, and labor bestowed upon them, not according to the rank and dignity of the persons represented. If a statue of Mercury cost less than one of Jupiter or Juno, it was because less skill, industry, and labor had been expended upon it. And such was the case here. The statues of Jupiter and Juno were full-length figures, while that of Mercury was a miserable square post, with only the head and shoulders of the god upon it. What wonder, then, that it might be thrown in without extra charge? Mercury overlooked this circumstance, from having in mind only his own fancied superiority, and his humiliation was therefore as natural as it was merited. We look in vain among the commentators, translators, and imitators of Æsop's fables for any trace of this explanation. I could mention the names of many, were it worth the trouble, who have understood the story literally; that is, have not understood it at all. On the supposition that the workmanship of all the statues was of the same degree of excellence, there is an absurdity in the fable which these scholars have either failed to perceive or have very much exaggerated. Another point which, perhaps, might be taken exception to in the fable, is the price the sculptor sets upon his Jupiter. No potter can make a puppet for a drachm. The drachm here must stand in general for something very insignificant. (Fab. Æsop, 90.)

NOTE 20, p. 53.

LUCRETIUS de R. N. lib. v. 736–747.

It Ver, et Venus, et Veneris prænuntius ante
Pinnatus graditur Zephyrus; vestigia propter
Flora quibus mater præspargens ante viai
Cuncta coloribus egregiis et odoribus opplet,
Inde loci sequitur Calor aridus, et comes una
Pulverulenta Ceres; et Etesia flabra Aquilonum.
Inde Autumnus adit; graditur simul Evius Evan;
Inde aliæ tempestates ventique sequuntur,
Altitonans Vulturnus et Auster fulmine pollens.

Tandem Bruma nives adfert, pigrumque rigorem
Reddit, Hyems sequitur, crepitans ac dentibus Algus.

Spring advances and Venus and winged Zephyrus, the herald of Venus, precedes, whose path mother Flora fills with wondrous flowers and odors. Then follow in order dry Heat and his companion dusty Ceres, and the Etesian blasts of the Northwind. Then Autumn approaches, and Evian Bacchus. Then other tempests and winds, deep-thundering Volturnus and Auster (south and south-east winds), mighty with lightnings. At length, the solstice brings snow, and slothful numbness returns; Winter follows, and cold with chattering teeth.

Spence regards this passage as one of the most beautiful in the whole poem, and it is certainly one on which the fame of Lucretius as a poet chiefly rests. But, surely, to say that the whole description was probably taken from a procession of statues representing the seasons as gods, is to detract very much from his merit, if not to destroy it altogether. And what reason have we for the supposition? This, says the Englishman: "Such processions of their deities in general were as common among the Romans of old, as those in honor of the saints are in the same country to this day. All the expressions used by Lucretius here come in very aptly, if applied to a procession."

Excellent reasons! Against the last, particularly, we might make many objections. The very epithets applied to the various personified abstractions,—"Calor aridus," "Ceres pulverulenta," "Volturnus altitonans," "fulmine pollens Auster," "Algus dentibus crepitans,"—show that they received their characteristics from the poet and not from the artist. He would certainly have treated them very differently. Spence seems to have derived his idea of a procession from Abraham Preigern, who, in his remarks on this passage, says, "Ordo est quasi Pompæ cujusdam. Ver et Venus, Zephyrus et Flora," &c. But Spence should have been content to stop there. To say that the poet makes his seasons move as in a procession, is all very well; but to say that he learned their sequences from a procession, is nonsense.

Note 21, p. 62.

Valerius Flaccus, lib. ii. Argonaut, v. 265–273.

> Serta patri, juvenisque comam vestisque Lyæi
> Induit, et medium curru locat; æraque circum
> Tympanaque et plenas tacita formidine cistas.
> Ipsa sinus hederisque ligat famularibus artus;
> Pampineamque quatit ventosis ictibus hastam,
> Respiciens; teneat virides velatus habenas
> Ut pater, et nivea tumeant ut cornua mitra,
> Et sacer ut Bacchum referat scyphus.

"The maid clothes her father with the garlands, the locks and the garments of Bacchus, and places him in the centre of the chariot; around him the brazen drums and the boxes filled with nameless terror; herself, looking back, binds his hair and limbs with ivy and strikes windy blows with the vine-wreathed spear; veiled like the father she holds the green reins; the horns project under the white turban, and the sacred goblet tells of Bacchus."

The word "tumeant," in the last line but one, would seem to imply that the horns were not so small as Spence fancies.

Note 22, p. 62.

The so-called Bacchus in the garden of the Medicis at Rome (Montfaucon Suppl. aux Ant. T. I, p. 254) has little horns growing from the brow. But for this very reason some critics suppose it to be a faun. And indeed such natural horns are an insult to the human countenance, and can only be becoming in beings supposed to occupy a middle station between men and beasts. The attitude also and the longing looks the figure casts upward at the grapes belong more properly to a follower of the god than to the god himself. I am reminded here of what Clemens Alexandrinus says of Alexander the Great. (Protrept. p. 48, edit. Pott.) *Ἐβούλετο δὲ καὶ Ἀλέξανδρος Ἄμμωνος υἱὸς εἶναι δοκεῖν, καὶ κεράσφορος ἀναπλάττεσθαι πρὸς τῶν ἀγαλματοποιῶν, τὸ καλὸν ἀνθρώπου ὑβρίσαι σπεύδων κέρατι.* It was Alexander's express desire to be represented in his statue with horns. He was well content with the insult thus done to human beauty, if only a divine origin might be imputed to him.

NOTE 23, p. 64.

WHEN I maintained in a former chapter that the old artists had never made a fury, it had not escaped me that the furies had more than one temple, which certainly would not have been left devoid of their statues. Pausanias found some of wood in their temple at Cerynea, not large nor in any way remarkable. It would seem that the art, which had no opportunity of displaying itself on them, sought to make amends on the images of the priestesses which stood in the hall of the temple, as they were of stone and of very beautiful workmanship. (Pausanias Achaic. cap. xxv. p. 587, edit. Kuhn.) Neither had I forgotten that heads of them were supposed to have been found on an *abraxas*, made known by Chiffletius, and on a lamp by Licetus. (Dissertat. sur les Furies par Bannier; Mémoires de l'Académie des Inscript. T. v. 48.) Neither was I unacquainted with the Etruscan vase of Gorius (Tabl. 151. Musei Etrusci) whereon are Orestes and Pylades attacked by furies. But I was speaking of works of art, under which head I consider none of these to come. If the latter deserve more than the others to be included under the name, it would in one aspect rather confirm my theory than contradict it. For, little as the Etruscan artists aimed at beauty in most cases, they yet seem to have characterized the furies more by their dress and attributes than by any terrible aspect of countenance. These figures thrust their torches at Orestes and Pylades, with such a tranquil expression of face that they almost seem to be terrifying them in sport. The horror they inspire in Orestes and Pylades appears from the fear of the two men, not at all from the shape of the furies themselves.

They are, therefore, at once furies and no furies. They perform the office of furies, but without that appearance of violence and rage which we are accustomed to associate with the name. They have not that brow which, as Catullus says, "expirantis præportat pectoris iras." Winkelmann though lately that he had discovered, upon a cornelian in the cabinet of Stoss, a fury, running, with streaming hair and garments, and a dagger in her hand. (Library of the Fine Arts, vol. v.) Von Hagedorn at once counselled all the artists to turn this discovery to account, and represent furies thus in their pictures. (Betrachtungen über die Malerei, p. 222.) But Winkelmann himself presently threw doubt on his discovery, because he did not find that the ancients ever armed the furies with daggers instead of torches. (Descript. des Pierres Gravées, p. 84.) He must then consider the figures on the coins of the cities of Lyrba and Massaura, which Spanheim calls furies (Les Césars de Julien, p. 44), to be not such but a Hecate *triformis*. Else here would be exactly such a fury, with a dagger in each hand, and strangely enough also with flowing hair, while in the other figures the hair is covered with a veil. But granting Winkelmann's first supposition to have been correct, the same would apply to this engraved stone as to the Etruscan vase, unless owing to the fineness of the work the features were indistinguishable. Besides, all engraved stones, from their use as seals, belong rather to symbolism; and the figures on them are more often a conceit of the owner than the voluntary work of the artist.

Note 24, p. 64.

Fast. lib. vi. 295–98.

> Esse diu stultus Vestæ simulacra putavi:
> Mox didici curvo nulla subesse tholo.
> Ignis inextinctus templo celatur in illo;
> Effigiem nullam Vesta, nec ignis, habet.

"I long foolishly thought there were images of Vesta; then I found that none existed beneath the arching dome. An ever-burning fire is hidden in that temple. Image there is none either of Vesta or of fire."

Ovid is speaking only of the worship of Vesta at Rome, and of the temple erected to her there by Numa, of whom he just before says:

> Regis opus placidi, quo non metuentius ullum
> Numinis ingenium terra Sabina tulit.

"The work of that peaceful king who feared the gods more than any other offspring of the Sabine land."

NOTE 25, p. 65.

FAST. lib. iii. v. 45, 46.

> Sylvia fit mater: Vestæ simulacra feruntur
> Virgineas oculis opposuisse manus.

Spence should thus have compared the different parts of Ovid together. The poet is speaking of different times; here of the state of things before Numa, there of the state of things after him. Statues of her were worshipped in Italy as they were in Troy, whence Æneas brought her rites with him.

> Manibus vittas, Vestamque potentem,
> Æternumque adytis effert penetralibus ignem,

says Virgil of the ghost of Hector, after he had warned Æneas to fly. "He bears in his hands from the innermost shrine garlands, and mighty Vesta and the eternal fire." Here the eternal fire is expressly distinguished from Vesta herself and from her statue. Spence cannot have consulted the Roman poets with much care, since he allowed such a passage as this to escape him.

NOTE 26, p. 65.

PLINIUS, lib. xxxvi. sect. 4. "Scopas fecit.—Vestam sedentem laudatam in Servilianis hortis." Lipsius must have had this passage in mind when he wrote (de Vesta cap. 3): "Plinius Vestem sedentem effingi solitam ostendit, a stabilitate." But what Pliny says of a single work by Scopas he ought not to have taken for a generally accepted characteristic. In fact, he observes that on coins Vesta was as often represented standing as sitting. This, however, was no correction of Pliny, but only of his own mistaken conception.

NOTE 27, p. 66.

GEORG. Codinus de Originib. Constant. *Τὴν γῆν λέγουσιν Ἑστίαν, καὶ πλάττουσιν αὐτὴν γυναῖκα, τύμπανον βαστάζουσαν, ἐπειδὴ τοὺς ἀνέμους ἡ γῆ ὑφ' ἑαυτὴν συγκλείει.* Suidas, following him, or both following some older authority, says the same thing under the word *Ἑστία.* "Under the name of Vesta the Earth is represented by a woman bearing a drum, in which she is supposed to hold the winds confined." The reason is somewhat puerile. It would have sounded better to say that she carried a drum, because the ancients thought her figure bore some resemblance to one, *σχῆμα αὐτῆς τυμπανοειδὲς εἶναι.* (Plutarchus de placitis Philos. cap. 10, id. de facie in orbe Lunæ.) Perhaps, after all, Codinus was mistaken in the figure or the name or both. Possibly he did not know what better name to give to what he saw Vesta holding, than a drum. Or he might have heard it called tympanum, and the only thing the word suggested to him was the instrument known to us as a kettle-drum. But "tympana" were also a kind of wheel.

> Hinc radios trivere rotis, hinc tympana plaustris
> Agricolæ. — (Virgilius Georgic. lib. ii. 444.)

Very similar to such a wheel appears to me the object borne by Fabretti's Vesta (ad Tabulam Iliadis, p. 334) which that scholar takes to be a hand-mill.

NOTE 28, p. 70.

LIB. i. Od. 35.

> Te semper anteit sæva Necessitas:
> Clavos trabales et cuneos manu
> Gestans ahenea; nec severus
> Uncus abest liquidumque plumbum.

In this picture of Necessity drawn by Horace, perhaps the richest in attributes of any to be found in the old poets, the nails, the clamps, and the liquid lead, whether regarded as means of confinement or implements of punishment, still belong to the class of poetical, rather than allegorical, attributes. But, even so, they are too crowded; and the passage is one of the least effective in Horace. Sanadon says: "J'ose dire que ce tableau, pris dans le détail, serait plus beau sur la toile que dans une ode héroïque. Je ne puis souffrir cet attirail patibulaire de clous, de coins, de crocs, et de plomb fondu. J'ai cru en devoir décharger la traduction, en susbtituant les idées générales aux idées singulières. C'est dommage que le poëte ait eu besoin de ce correctif." Sanadon's sentiment was fine and true, but he does not give the right ground for it. The objection is not that these attributes are the paraphernalia of the gallows, for he had but to interpret them in their other sense to make them the firmest supports of architecture. Their fault is in being addressed to the eye and not to the ear. For all impressions meant for the eye, but presented to us through the ear, are received with effort, and produce no great degree of vividness. These lines of Horace remind me of a couple of oversights on the part of Spence, which give us no very good idea of the exactitude with which he has studied the passages he cites from the old poets. He is speaking of the image under which the Romans represented faith or honesty. (Dial. x.) "The Romans," he says, "called her 'Fides;' and, when they called her 'Sola Fides,' seem to mean the same as we do by the words 'downright honesty.' She is represented with an erect, open air, and with nothing but a thin robe on, so fine that one might see through it. Horace therefore calls her 'thin-dressed' in one of his odes, and 'transparent' in another." In these few lines are not less than three gross errors. First, it is false that "sola" was a distinct epithet applied to the goddess Fides. In the two passages from Livy, which he adduces as proof (lib. i. sect. 21, lib. ii. sect. 3), the word has only its usual signification, — the exclusion of all else. In one place, indeed, the "soli" has been questioned by the critics, who think it must have crept into the text through an error in writing, occasioned by the word next to it, which is "solenne." In the other passage cited, the author is not speaking of fidelity at all, but of innocence, Innocentia. Secondly, Horace, in one of his odes (the thirty-fifth of the first book, mentioned above), is said to have applied to Fides the epithet thin-dressed:

> Te spes, et albo rara fides colit
> Velata panno.

"Rarus," it is true, can also mean thin; but here it means only rare, seldom appearing, and is applied to Fidelity herself, not to her clothing. Spence would have been right, had the poet said, "Fides raro velata panno." Thirdly, Horace is said to have elsewhere called faith or honesty transparent, in the sense in which friends protest to one another, "I wish you could read my heart." This meaning is said to be found in the line of the eighteenth ode of the First Book:

> Arcanique Fides prodiga, pellucidior vitro.

How can a critic allow himself to be thus misled by a word? Is a faith, "arcani prodiga," lavish of secrets, faithfulness? is it not rather faithlessness? And it is of faithlessness, in fact, that Horace says, "She is transparent as glass, because she betrays to every eye the secrets entrusted to her."

NOTE 29, p. 71.

APOLLO delivers the washed and embalmed body of Sarpedon to Death and Sleep, that they may bring him to his native country. (Iliad, xvi. 681, 682.)

> *πέμπε δέ μιν πομποῖσιν ἅμα κραιπνοῖσι φέρεσθαι,*
> *Ὕπνῳ καὶ Θανάτῳ διδυμάοσιν.*

Caylus recommends this idea to the painter, but adds: "It is a pity that Homer has given us no account of the attributes under which Sleep was represented in his day. We recognize the god only by his act, and we crown him with poppies. These ideas are modern. The first is of service, but cannot be employed in the present case, where even the flowers would be out of keeping in connection with the figure of Death." (Tableaux tirés de l'Iliade, de l'Odyssée d'Homère, et de l'Enéide de Virgile, avec des observations générales sur le costume, à Paris, 1757–58.) That is requiring of Homer ornamentations of that petty kind most at variance with the nobility of his style. The most ingenious attributes he could have bestowed on Sleep would not have characterized him so perfectly, nor have brought so vivid a picture of him before us, as the single touch which makes him the twin brother of Death. Let the artist seek to express this, and he may dispense with all attributes. The old artists did, in fact, make Sleep and Death resemble each other, like twin-brothers. On a chest of cedar, in the Temple of Juno at Elis, they both lay as boys in the arms of Night. One was white, the other black; one slept, the other only seemed to sleep; the feet of both were crossed. For so I should prefer to translate the words of Pausanias (Eliac. cap. xviii. p. 422, edit. Kuhn), *ἀμφοτέρους διεστραμμένους τοὺς πόδας*, rather than by "crooked feet," as Gedoyn does, "les pieds contrefaits." What would be the meaning of crooked feet? To lie with crossed feet is customary with sleepers. Sleep is thus represented by Maffei. (Raccol. Pl. 151.) Modern artists have entirely abandoned this resemblance between Sleep and Death, which we find among the ancients, and always represent Death as a skeleton, or at best a skeleton covered with skin. Caylus should have been careful to tell the artists whether they had better follow the custom of the ancients or the moderns in this respect. He seems to declare in favor of the modern view, since he regards Death as a figure that would not harmonize well with a flower-crowned companion. Has he further considered how inappropriate this modern idea would be in a Homeric picture? How could its loathsome character have failed to shock him? I cannot bring myself to believe that the little metal figure in the ducal gallery at Florence, representing a skeleton sitting on the ground, with one arm on an urn of ashes (Spence's Polymetis, tab. xli.), is a veritable antique. It cannot possibly represent Death, because the ancients represented him very differently. Even their poets never thought of him under this repulsive shape.

NOTE 30, p. 76.

RICHARDSON cites this work as an illustration of the rule that the attention of the spectator should be diverted by nothing, however admirable, from the chief figure. "Protogenes," he says, "had introduced into his famous picture of Ialysus a partridge, painted with so much skill that it seemed alive, and was admired by all Greece. But, because it attracted all eyes to itself, to the detriment of the whole piece, he effaced it." (Traité de la Peinture, T. i. p. 46.) Richardson is mistaken; this partridge was not in the Ialysus, but in another picture of Protogenes called the Idle Satyr, or Satyr in Repose, *Σάτυρος ἀναπαυόμενος*. I should hardly have mentioned this error, which arose from a misunderstanding of a passage in Pliny, had not the same mistake been made by Meursius. (Rhodi. lib. i. cap. 14.) "In eadem tabula, scilicet in qua Ialysus, Satyrus erat, quem dicebant *Anapauomenon*, tibeas tenens."

Something of the same kind occurs in Winkelmann. (Von der Nachahm. der Gr. W. in der Mal. und Bildh. p. 56.) Strabo is the only authority for this partridge story, and he expressly discriminates between the Ialysus and the Satyr leaning against a pillar on which sat the partridge. (Lib. xiv.) Meursius, Richardson, and Winkelmann misunderstood the passage in Pliny (lib. xxxv. sect. 36), from not perceiving that he was speaking of two different pictures: the one which saved the city, because Demetrius would not assault the place where it stood; and another, which Protogenes painted during the siege. The one was Ialysus, the other the Satyr.

NOTE 31, p. 79.

THIS invisible battle of the gods has been imitated by Quintus Calaber in his Twelfth Book, with the evident design of improving on his model. The grammarian seems to have held it unbecoming in a god to be thrown to the ground by a stone. He therefore makes the gods hurl at one another huge masses of rock, torn up from Mount Ida, which, however, are shattered against the limbs of the immortals and fly like sand about them.

. . . οἱ δὲ κολώνας
χερσὶν ἀποῤῥήξαντες ἀπ' οὔδεος 'Ιδαίοιο
βάλλον ἐπ' ἀλλήλους· αἱ δε ψαμάθοισι ὅμοιαι
ῥεῖα διεοκίδναντο θεῶν περὶ δ' ἄσχετα γυῖα
ῥηγνύμενα διὰ τυτθα. . . .

A conceit which destroys the effect by marring our idea of the size of the gods, and throwing contempt on their weapons. If gods throw stones at one another, the stones must be able to hurt them, or they are like silly boys pelting each other with earth. So old Homer remains still the wiser, and all the fault-finding of cold criticism, and the attempts of men of inferior genius to vie with him, serve but to set forth his wisdom in clearer light. I do not deny that Quintus's imitation has excellent and original points; but they are less in harmony with the modest greatness of Homer than calculated to do honor to the stormy fire of a more modern poet. That the cry of the gods, which rang to the heights of heaven and the depths of hell, should not be heard by mortals, seems to me a most expressive touch. The cry was too mighty to be grasped by the imperfect organs of human hearing.

NOTE 32, p. 80.

No one who has read Homer once through, ever so hastily, will differ from this statement as far as regards strength and speed; but he will not perhaps at once recall examples where the poet attaches superhuman size to his gods. I would therefore refer him, in addition to the description of Mars just quoted, whose body covered seven hides, to the helmet of Minerva, *κυνέην ἑπατὸν πολίων πρυλέεσσ' ἀραρυῖαν* (Iliad, v. 744), under which could be concealed as many warriors as a hundred cities could bring into the field; to the stride of Neptune (Iliad, xiii. 20); and especially to the lines from the description of the shield, where Mars and Minerva lead the troops of the beleaguered city. (Iliad, xviii. 516–519.)

ἦρχε δ' ἄρα σφιν Ἄρης καὶ Παλλὰς Ἀθήνη,
ἄμφω χρυσείω, χρύσεια δὲ εἵματα ἕσθην,
καλὼ καὶ μεγάλω σὺν τεύχεσιν, ὥστε θεώ περ,
ἀμφὶς ἀριζήλω· λαοὶ δ' ὑπ' ὀλίζονες ἦσαν.

. . . While the youths
Marched on, with Mars and Pallas at their head,
Both wrought in gold, with golden garments on,

Stately and large in form, and over all
Conspicuous in bright armor, as became
Th gods; the rest were of an humbler size. — BRYANT.

Judging from the explanations they feel called upon to give of the great helmet of Minerva, Homer's commentators, old as well as new, seem not always sufficiently to have borne in mind this wonderful size of the gods. (See the notes on the above-quoted passage in the edition of Clarke and Ernesti.) But we lose much in majesty by thinking of the Homeric deities as of ordinary size, as we are accustomed to see them on canvas in the company of mortals. Although painting is unable to represent these superhuman dimensions, sculpture to a certain extent may, and I am convinced that the old masters borrowed from Homer their conception of the gods in general as well as the colossal size which they not infrequently gave them. (Herodot. lib. ii. p. 130, edit. Wessel.) Further remarks upon the use of the colossal, its excellent effect in sculpture and its want of effect in painting, I reserve for another place.

NOTE 33, p. 82.

HOMER, I acknowledge, sometimes veils his deities in a cloud, but only when they are not to be seen by other deities. In the fourteenth book of the Iliad, for instance, where Juno and Sleep, *ἠέρα ἑσσαμένω*, betake themselves to Mount Ida, the crafty goddess's chief care was not to be discovered by Venus, whose girdle she had borrowed under pretence of a very different journey. In the same book the love-drunken Jupiter is obliged to surround himself and his spouse with a golden cloud to overcome her chaste reluctance.

πῶς κ' ἔοι, εἴ τις νῶϊ θεῶν αἰειγενετάων
εὕδοντ' ἀθρήσειε. . . .

She did not fear to be seen by men, but by the gods. And although Homer makes Jupiter say a few lines further on, —

Ἥρη, μήτε θεῶν τόγε δείδιθι μήτε τιν' ἀνδρῶν
ὄψεσθαι· τοῖόν τοι ἐγὼ νέφος ἀμφικαλύψω,
χρύσεον.

"Fear thou not that any god or man will look upon us," that does not prove that the cloud was needed to conceal them from the eyes of mortals, but that in this cloud they would be as invisible to the gods as they always were to men. So, when Minerva puts on the helmet of Pluto (Iliad, v. 485), which has the same effect of concealment that a cloud would have, it is not that she may be concealed from the Trojans, who either see her not at all or under the form of Sthenelus, but simply that she may not be recognized by Mars.

NOTE 34, p. 87.

TABLEAUX tirés de l'Iliade, Avert. p. 5. "On est toujours convenu, que plus un poëme fournissait d'images et d'actions, plus il avait de supériorité en poésie. Cette réflexion m'avait conduit à penser que le calcul des différens tableaux, qu' offrent les poëmes, pouvait servir à comparer le mérite respectif des poëmes et des poëtes. Le nombre et le genre des tableaux que présentent ces grands ouvrages, auraient été une espèce de pierre de touche, ou, plutôt, une balance certaine du mérite de ces poëmes et du génie de leurs auteurs."

NOTE 35, p. 88.

WHAT we call poetic pictures, the ancients, as we learn from Longinus, called "phantasiæ;" and what we call illusion in such pictures, they named "enargia." It was therefore said by some one, as Plutarch tells us (Erot. T. ii. edit. Henr. Steph. p. 1351), that poetic "phantasiæ" were, on account of their "enargia," waking dreams: *Αἱ ποιητικαὶ φαντασίαι διὰ τὴν ἐνάργειαν ἐγρηγορότων ἐνύπνια εἰσίν.* I could wish that our modern books upon poetry had used this nomenclature, and avoided the word picture altogether. We should thus have been spared a multitude of doubtful rules, whose chief foundation is the coincidence of an arbitrary term. No one would then have thought of confining poetic conceptions within the limits of a material picture. But the moment these conceptions were called a poetic picture, the foundation for the error was laid.

NOTE 36, p. 89.

ILIAD, iv. 105.

αὐτίκ' ἐσύλα τόξον ἐΰξοον
καὶ τὸ μὲν εὖ κατέθηκε τανυσσάμενος, ποτὶ γαίῃ
ἀγκλίνας· . . .
αὐτὰρ ὁ σύλα πῶμα φαρέτρης, ἐκ δ' ἕλετ' ἰὸν
ἀβλῆτα πτερόεντα, μελαινέων ἕρμ' ὀδυνάων·
αἶψα δ' ἐπὶ νευρῇ κατεκόσμει πικρὸν ὀϊστὸν,
ἕλκε δ' ὁμοῦ γλυφίδας τε λαβὼν καὶ νεῦρα βόεια·
νευρὴν μὲν μαζῷ πέλασεν, τόξον δέ σίδηρον.
αὐτὰρ ἐπειδὴ κυκλοτερὲς μέγα τόξον ἔτεινεν,
λίγξε βιὸς, νευρὴ δὲ μέγ' ἴαχεν ἆλτο δ' ὀϊστὸς
ὀξυβελὴς, καθ' ὅμιλον ἐπιπτέσθαι μενεαίνων.

To bend that bow the warrior lowered it
And pressed an end against the earth. . . .
Then the Lycian drew aside
The cover from his quiver, taking out
A well-fledged arrow that had never flown,—
A cause of future sorrows. On the string
He laid that fatal arrow. . . .
Grasping the bowstring and the arrow's notch
He drew them back and forced the string to meet
His breast, the arrow-head to meet the bow,
Till the bow formed a circle. Then it twanged;
The cord gave out a shrilly sound; the shaft
Leaped forth in eager haste to reach the host.—BRYANT.

NOTE 37, p. 108.

PROLOGUE to the Satires, 340.

That not in Fancy's maze he wandered long,
But stooped to Truth and moralized his song.

Ibid. 148.

. . . Who could take offence
While pure description held the place of sense?

Warburton's remark on this last line may have the force of an explanation by the poet himself. "He uses *pure* equivocally, to signify either chaste or empty; and has given in this line what he esteemed the true character of descriptive poetry, as it is called, — a composition, in his opinion, as absurd as a feast made up of sauces. The use of a picturesque imagination is to brighten and adorn good sense: so that to employ it only in description, is like children's delighting in a prism for the sake of its gaudy colors, which, when frugally managed and artfully disposed, might be made to represent and illustrate the noblest objects in nature."

Both poet and commentator seem to have regarded the matter rather from a moral than an artistic point of view. But so much the better that this style of poetry seems equally worthless from whichever point it be viewed.

NOTE 38, p. 108.

POETIQUE Française, T. ii. p. 501. "J'écrivais ces réflexions avant que les essais des Allemands dans ce genre (l'Eglogue) fussent connus parmi nous. Ils ont exécuté ce que j'avais conçu; et s'ils parviennent à donner plus au moral et moins au détail des peintures physiques, ils excelleront dans ce genre, plus riche, plus vaste, plus fécond, et infiniment plus naturel et plus moral que celui de la galanterie champêtre.

NOTE 39, p. 115.

I SEE that Servius attempts to excuse Virgil on other grounds, for the difference between the two shields has not escaped his notice. "Sane interest inter hunc et Homeri clypeum; illic enim singula dum fiunt narrantur; hic vero perfecto opere nascuntur; nam et hic arma prius accipit Æneas, quam spectaret; ibi postquam omnia narrata sunt, sic a Thetide deferuntur ad Achillem." There is a marked difference between this and the shield of Homer: for there events are narrated one by one as they are done, here they are known by the finished work; here the arms are received by Æneas before being seen, there, after all has been told, they are carried by Thetis to Achilles. (Ad. v. 625, lib. viii. Æneid.) Why? "For this reason," says Servius: "because, on the shield of Æneas, were represented not only the few events referred to by the poet, but, —

. . . genus omne futuræ
Stirpis ab Ascanio, pugnataque in ordine bella,

"All the description of his future race from Ascanius, and the battles, in the order in which they should occur." It would have been impossible for the poet, in the same short space of time occupied by Vulcan in his work, to mention by name the long line of descendants, and to tell of all their battles in the order of their occurrence. That seems to be the meaning of Servius's somewhat obscure words: "Opportune ergo Virgilius, quia non videtur simul et narrationis celeritas potuisse connecti, et opus tam velociter expedire, ut ad verbum posset occurrere." Since Virgil could bring forward but a small part of "the unnarratable text of the shield," and not even that little while Vulcan was at work, he was obliged to reserve it till the whole was finished. For Virgil's sake, I hope that this argument of Servius is baseless. My excuse is much more creditable to him. What need was there of putting the whole of Roman history on a shield? With few pictures Homer made his shield an epitome of all that was happening in the world. It would almost seem that Virgil, despairing of surpassing the Greek in the design and execution of his pictures, was determined to exceed him at least in their number, and that would have been the height of childishness.

NOTE 40, p. 118.

"SCUTO ejus, in quo Amazonum prœlium cælavit intumescente ambitu parmæ; ejusdem concava parte deorum et gigantum, dimicationem."

"Her shield, on the convex side of which he sculptured a battle of the Amazons, and on the concave side the contest of the gods and giants." (Plinius, lib. xxxvi. sect. 4.)

NOTE 41, p. 122.

THE first begins at line 483 and goes to line 489; the second extends from 490 to 509; the third, from 510 to 540; the fourth, from 541 to 549; the fifth, from 550 to 560; the sixth, from 561 to 572; the seventh, from 573 to 586; the eighth, from 587 to 589; the ninth, from 590 to 605; and the tenth, from 606 to 608. The third picture alone is not so introduced; but that it is one by itself is evident from the words introducing the second, — ἐν δὲ δύω ποίησε πόλεις, — as also from the nature of the subject.

NOTE 42, p. 123.

ILIAD, vol. v. obs. p. 61. In this passage Pope makes an entirely false use of the expression "aerial perspective," which, in fact, has nothing to do with the diminishing of the size according to the increased distance, but refers only to the change of color occasioned by the air or other medium through which the object is seen. A man capable of this blunder may justly be supposed ignorant of the whole subject.

NOTE 43, p. 128.

CONSTANTINUS Manasses Compend. Chron. p. 20 (edit. Venet). Madame Dacier was well pleased with this portrait of Manasses, except for its tautology. "De Helenæ pulchritudine omnium optime Constantinus Manasses; nisi in eo tautologiam reprehendas. (Ad Dictyn Cretensem, lib. i. cap. 3, p. 5.) She also quotes, according to Mezeriac (Comment. sur les Epîtres d'Ovide, T. i. p. 361), the descriptions given by Dares Phrygius, and Cedrenus, of the beauty of Helen. In the first there is one trait which sounds rather strange. Dares says that Helen had a mole between her eyebrows: "notam inter duo supercilia habentem." But that could not have been a beauty. I wish the Frenchwoman had given her opinion. I, for my part, regard the word "nota" as a corruption, and think that Dares meant to speak of what the Greeks called *μεσόφρυον*, and the Latins, "glabella." He means to say that Helen's eyebrows did not meet, but that there was a little space between them. The taste of the ancients was divided on this point. Some considered this space between the eyebrows beauty, others not. (Junius de Pictura Vet. lib. iii. cap. 9, p. 245.) Anacreon took a middle course. The eyebrows of his beloved maiden were neither perceptibly separated, nor were they fully grown together: they tapered off delicately at a certain point. He says to the artist who is to paint her (Od. 28): —

> τὸ μεσόφρυον δὲ μέ μοι
> διάκοπτε, μήτε μίσγε,
> ἐχέτω δ' ὅπως ἐκείνη
> τὶ λεληθότως σύνοφρυν
> βλεφάρων ἴτυν κελαινήν.

This is Pauer's reading, but the meaning is the same in other versions, and has been rightly given by Henr. Stephano: —

> Supercilii nigrantes
> Discrimina nec arcus,
> Confundito nec illos:
> Sed junge sic ut anceps
> Divortium relinquas,
> Quale esse cernis ipsi.

But if my interpretation of Dares' meaning be the true one, what should we read instead of "notam?" Perhaps "moram." For certainly "mora" may mean not only the interval of time before something happens, but also the impediment, the space between one thing and another.

> Ego inquieta montium jaceam mora,

is the wish of the raving Hercules in Seneca, which Gronovius very well explains thus: "Optat se medium jacere inter duas Symplegades, illarum velut moram, impedimentum, obicem; qui eas moretur, vetet aut satis arcte conjungi, aut rursus distrahi." The same poet uses "laceratorum moræ" in the sense of "juncturæ." (Schrœderus ad. v. 762. Thyest.)

NOTE 44, p. 131.

DIALOGO della Pittura, intitolata l' Aretino: Firenze 1735, p. 178. "Se vogliono i Pittori senza fatica trovare un perfetto esempio di bella Donna, legiano quelle Stanze dell' Ariosto, nelle quali egli discrive mirabilmente le belezze della Fata Alcina; e vedranno parimente, quanto i buoni Poeti siano ancora essi Pittori."

NOTE 45, p. 131.

IBID. "Ecco, che, quanto alla proporzione, l' ingeniosissimo Ariosto assegna la migliore, che sappiano formar le mani de' più eccellenti Pittori, usando questa voce industri, per dinotar la diligenza, che conviene al buono artefice."

NOTE 46, p. 132.

IBID. "Qui l' Ariosto colorisce, e in questo suo colorire dimostra essere un Titiano."

NOTE 47, p. 132.

IBID. "Poteva l' Ariosto nella guisa, che ha detto chioma bionda, dir chioma d' oro: ma gli parve forse, che havrebbe havuto troppo del Poetico. Da che si può ritrar, che 'l Pittore dee imitar l 'oro, e non metterlo (come fanno i Miniatori) nelle sue Pitture, in modo, che si possa dire, que capelli non sono d' oro, ma par che risplendano, come l' oro." What Dolce goes on to quote from Athenæus is remarkable, but happens to be a misquotation. I shall speak of it in another place.

NOTE 48, p. 132.

IBID. "Il naso, che discende giù, havendo peraventura la considerazione a quelle forme de' nasi, che si veggono ne' ritratti delle belle Romane antiche."

NOTE 49, p. 143.

PLINY says of Apelles (lib. xxxv. sect. 36): "Fecit et Dianam sacrificantium Virginum choro mixtam; quibus vicisse Homeri versus videtur id ipsum describentis." "He also made a Diana surrounded by a band of virgins performing a sacrifice; a work in which he would seem to have surpassed the verses of Homer describing the same thing." This praise may be perfectly just; for beautiful nymphs surrounding a beautiful goddess, who towers above them by the whole height of her majestic brow, form a theme more fitting the painter than the poet. But I am somewhat suspicious of the word "sacrifican tium." What have the nymphs of Diana to do with offering sacrifices? Is that the occupation assigned them by Homer? By no means. They roam with the goddess over hills and through forest; they hunt, play, dance. (Odyss. vi. 102–106).

> οἵη δ' Ἄρτεμις εἶσι κατ' οὔρεος ἰοχέαιρα
> ἢ κατὰ Τηΰγετον περιμήκετον, ἢ Ἐρύμανθον
> τερπομένη κάπροισι καὶ ὠκείῃς ἐλάφοισι·
> τῇ δέ θ' ἅμα Νύμφαι, κοῦραι Διὸς αἰγιόχοιο
> ἀγρονόμοι παίζουσι· . . .

> As when o'er Erymanth Diana roves
> Or wide Taygetus's resounding groves;
> A sylvan train the huntress queen surrounds,
> Her rattling quiver from her shoulder sounds;
> Fierce in the sport along the mountain brow,
> They bay the boar or chase the bounding roe.
> High o'er the lawn with more majestic pace,
> Above the nymphs she treads with stately grace. — Pope.

Pliny, therefore, can hardly have written "sacrificantium," rather "venantium" (hunting), or something like it; perhaps "sylvis vagantium" (roaming the woods), which corresponds more nearly in number of letters to the altered word. "Saltantium" (bounding), approaches most nearly to the *παίζουσι* of Homer. Virgil, also, in his imitation of this passage, represents the nymphs as dancing. (Æneid, i. 497, 498.)

> Qualis in Eurotæ ripis, aut per juga Cynthi
> Exercet Diana choros . . .
>
> Such on Eurotas' banks or Cynthus' height
> Diana seems; and so she charms the sight,
> When in the dance the graceful goddess leads
> The choir of nymphs and overtops their heads. — Dryden.

Spence gives a remarkable criticism on this passage. (Polymetis, dial. viii.) "This Diana," he says, "both in the picture and in the descriptions, was the Diana Venatrix, though she was not represented, either by Virgil or Apelles or Homer, as hunting with her nymphs; but as employed with them in that sort of dances which of old were regarded as very solemn acts of devotion." In a note he adds, "The expression of *παίζειν*, used by Homer on this occasion, is scarce proper for hunting; as that of "choros exercere," in Virgil, should be understood of the religious dances of old, because dancing, in the old Roman idea of it, was indecent, even for men, in public, unless it were the sort of dances used in honor of Mars or Bacchus or some other of their gods." Spence supposes that those solemn dances are here referred to, which, among the ancients, were counted among the acts of religion. "It is in consequence of this," he says, "that Pliny, in speaking of Diana's nymphs on this very occasion, uses the word "sacrificare" of them, which quite determines these dances of theirs to have been of the religious kind." He forgets that, in Virgil, Diana joins in the dance, "exercet Diana choros." If this were a religious dance, in whose honor did Diana dance it? in her own, or in honor of some other deity? Both suppositions are absurd. If the old Romans did hold dancing in general to be unbecoming in a grave person, was that a reason why their poets should transfer the national gravity to the manners of the gods, which were very differently represented by the old Greek poets? When Horace says of Venus (Od. iv. lib. i.),—

> Jam Cytherea choros ducit Venus, imminente luna;
> Junctæque Nymphis Gratiæ decentes
> Alterno terram quatiunt pede . . .

"Now Cytherean Venus leads the bands, under the shining moon, and the fair graces, joined with the nymphs, beat the ground with alternate feet,"—were these, likewise, sacred, religious dances? But it is wasting words to argue against such a conceit.

NOTE 50, p. 145.

PLINIUS, lib. xxxiv. sect. 19. "Ipse tamen corporum tenus curiosus, animi sensus non expressisse videtur, capillum quoque et pubem non emendatius fecisse, quam rudis antiquitas instituisset.

"Hic primus nervos et venas expressit, capillumque diligentius."

NOTE 51, p. 162.

THE Connoisseur, vol. i. no. 21. The beauty of Knonmquaiha is thus described. "He was struck with the glossy hue of her complexion, which shone like the jetty down on the black hogs of Hessaqua; he was ravished with the prest gristle of her nose; and his eyes dwelt with admiration on the flaccid beauties of her breasts, which descended to her navel." And how were these charms set off by art? "She made a varnish of the fat of goats mixed with soot, with which she anointed her whole body as she stood beneath the rays of the sun; her locks were clotted with melted grease, and powdered with the yellow dust of Buchu; her face, which shone like the polished ebony, was beautifully varied with spots of red earth, and appeared like the sable curtain of the night bespangled with stars; she sprinkled her limbs with wood-ashes, and perfumed them with the dung of Stinkbingsem. Her arms and legs were entwined with the shining entrails of an heifer; from her neck there hung a pouch composed of the stomach of a kid; the wings of an ostrich overshadowed the fleshy promontories behind; and before she wore an apron formed of the shaggy ears of a lion."

Here is further the marriage ceremony of the loving pair. "The Surri, or Chief Priest, approached them, and, in a deep voice, chanted the nuptial rites to the melodious grumbling of the Gom-Gom; and, at the same time (according to the manner of Caffraria), bedewed them plentifully with the urinary benediction. The bride and bridegroom rubbed in the precious stream with ecstasy, while the briny drops trickled from their bodies, like the oozy surge from the rocks of Chirigriqua."

NOTE 52, p. 166.

THE Sea-Voyage, act iii. scene 1. A French pirate ship is thrown upon a desert island. Avarice and envy cause quarrels among the men, and a couple of wretches, who had long suffered extreme want on the island, seize a favorable opportunity to put to sea in the ship. Robbed thus of their whole stock of provisions, the miserable men see death, in its worst forms, staring them in the face, and express to each other their hunger and despair as follows : —

> *Lamure*. Oh, what a tempest have I in my stomach!
> How my empty guts cry out! My wounds ache,
> Would they would bleed again, that I might get
> Something to quench my thirst!
> *Franville*. O Lamure, the happiness my dogs had
> When I kept house at home! They had a storehouse,
> A storehouse of most blessed bones and crusts.
> Happy crusts! Oh, how sharp hunger pinches me!
> *Lamure*. How now, what news?
> *Morillar*. Hast any meat yet?
> *Franville*. Not a bit that I can see.
> Here be goodly quarries, but they be cruel hard
> To gnaw. I ha' got some mud, we'll eat it with spoons;
> Very good thick mud; but it stinks damnably.
> There's old rotten trunks of trees, too,
> But not a leaf nor blossom in all the island.
> *Lamure*. How it looks!
> *Morillar*. It stinks too.
> *Lamure*. It may be poison.
> *Franville*. Let it be any thing,
> So I can get it down. Why, man,
> Poison's a princely dish!
> *Morillar*. Hast thou no biscuit?
> No crumbs left in thy pocket? Here is my doublet,
> Give me but three small crumbs.
> *Franville*. Not for three kingdoms,
> If I were master of 'em. Oh, Lamure,
> But one poor joint of mutton we ha' scorned, man!
> *Lamure*. Thou speak'st of paradise;
> Or but the snuffs of those healths,
> We have lewdly at midnight flung away.
> *Morillar*. Ah, but to lick the glasses!

But this is nothing, compared with the next scene, when the ship's surgeon enters.

> *Franville*. Here comes the surgeon. What
> Hast thou discovered? Smile, smile, and comfort us.

Surgeon. I am expiring,
Smile they that can. I can find nothing, gentlemen,
Here's nothing can be meat without a miracle.
Oh, that I had my boxes and my lints now,
My stupes, my tents, and those sweet helps of nature!
What dainty dishes could I make of them!
Morillar. Hast ne'er an old suppository?
Surgeon. Oh, would I had, sir!
Lamure. Or but the paper where such a cordial,
Potion, or pills hath been entombed!
Franville. Or the best bladder, where a cooling glister?
Morillar. Hast thou no searcloths left?
Nor any old poultices?
Franville. We care not to what it hath been ministered.
Surgeon. Sure I have none of these dainties, gentlemen.
Franville. Where's the great wen
Thou cut'st from Hugh the sailor's shoulder?
That would serve now for a most princely banquet.
Surgeon. Ay, if we had it, gentlemen.
I flung it overboard, slave that I was.
Lamure. A most improvident villain!

NOTE 53, p. 177.

ÆNEID, lib. ii. 7, and especially lib. xi. 183. We might safely, therefore, add such a work to the list of lost writings by this author.

NOTE 54, p. 179.

CONSULT the list of inscriptions on ancient works of art in Mar. Gudius. (ad Phædri fab. v. lib. i.), and, in connection with that, the correction made by Gronovius. (Præf. ad Tom. ix. Thesauri Antiq. Græc.)

NOTE 55, p. 182.

HE at least expressly promises to do so: "quæ suis locis reddam" (which I shall speak of in their proper place). But if this was not wholly forgotten, it was at least done very cursorily, and not at all in the way this promise had led us to expect. When he writes (lib. xxxv. sect. 39), "Lysippus quoque Æginæ picturæ suæ inscripsit, ἐνέκαυσεν; quod profecto non fecisset, nisi encaustica inventa," he evidently uses ἐνέκαυσεν to prove something quite different. If he meant, as Hardouin supposes, to indicate in this passage one of the works whose inscription was written in definite past time, it would have been worth his while to put in a word to that effect. Hardouin finds reference to the other two works in the following passage: "Idem (Divus Augustus) in Curia quoque, quam in Comitio consecrabat, duas tabulas impressit parieti: Nemeam sedentem supra leonem, palmigeram ipsam, adstante cum baculo sene, cujus supra caput tabula bigæ dependet. Nicias scripsit se inussisse; tali enim usus est verbo. Alterius tabulæ admiratio est, puberem filium seni patri similem esse, salva ætatis differentia, supervolante aquila draconem complexa. Philochares hoc suum opus esse testatus est." (Lib. xxxv. sect. 10.) Two different pictures are here described which Augustus had set up in the newly built senate-house. The second was by Philochares, the first by Nicias. All that is said of the picture by Philochares is plain and clear, but there are certain difficulties in regard to the other. It represented Nemea seated on a lion, a palm-branch in her hand, and near her an old man with a staff: "cujus supra caput tabula bigæ dependet." What is the meaning of that? "over his head hung a tablet on which was painted a two-horse chariot." That is the only meaning the words will bear. Was there, then, a smaller picture hung over the large one? and were both by Nicias? Hardouin must so have understood it, else where were the two pictures by Nicias, since the other is expressly ascribed to Philochares? "Inscripsit Nicias igitur geminæ huic tabulæ suum nomen in hunc modum: 'ΟΝΙΚΙΑΣ ΕΝΕΚΑΥΣΕΝ: atque adeo e tribus operibus, quæ absolute fuisse inscripta, ILLE FECIT, indicavit Præfatio ad Titum, duo hæc sunt Niciæ." I should like to ask Hardouin one question. If Nicias had really used the indefinite, and not the definite past tense, and Pliny had merely wished to say that the master, instead of *γράφειν*, had used *ἐγκαίειν*, would he not still have been obliged to say in Latin, "Nicias scripsit se inussisse?" But I will not insist upon this point. Pliny may really have meant to indicate here one of the three works before referred to. But who will be induced to believe that there were two pictures, placed one above the other? Not I for one. The words "cujus supra caput tabula bigæ dependet" must be a corruption. "Tabula bigæ," a picture of a two-horse chariot, does not sound much like Pliny, although Pliny does elsewhere use "biga" in the singular. What sort of a two-horse chariot? Such as were used in the races at the Nemæan games, so that this little picture should, from its subject, be related to the chief one? That cannot be; for not two but four horse chariots were usual in the Nemæan games. (Schmidius in Prol. ad Nemeonicas, p. 2.) At one time, I thought that Pliny might, instead of "bigæ," have written a Greek word, *πτυχίον*, which the copyists did not understand. For we know, from a passage in Antigonus Carystius, quoted by Zenobius (conf. Gronovius, T. ix. Antiquit. Græc. Præf. p. 7), that the old artists did not always put their name on the work itself, but sometimes on a separate tablet, attached to the picture or statue, and this tablet was called *πτυχίον*. The word "tabula, tabella," might have been written in the margin in explanation of the Greek word, and at last have crept into the text. *πτυχίον* was turned into "bigæ," and so we get "tabula bigæ." This *πτυχίον* agrees perfectly with what follows; for the next sentence contains what was written on it. The whole passage would then read thus: "cujus supra caput *πτυχίον* dependet, quo Nicias scripsit se inussisse." My correction is rather a bold one, I acknowledge. Need a critic feel obliged to suggest the proper reading for every passage that he can prove to be corrupted? I will rest content with having done the latter, and leave the former to some more skilful hand. But to return to the subject under discussion. If Pliny be here speaking of but a single picture by Nicias, on which he had inscribed his name in definite past time, and if the second picture thus inscribed be the abovementioned one of Lysippus, where is the third? That I cannot tell. If I might look for it elsewhere among the old writers, the question were easily answered. But it ought to be found in Pliny; and there, I repeat, I am entirely unable to discover it.

NOTE 56, p. 186.

THUS Statius says "obnixa pectora" (Thebaid. lib. vi. v. 863):

> . . . rumpunt obnixa furentes
> Pectora.

which the old commentator of Barths explains by "summa vi contra nitentia." Thus Ovid says (Halievt. v. ii.), "obnixa fronte," when describing the "scarus" trying to force its way through the fish-trap, not with his head, but with his tail.

> Non audet radiis obnixa occurrere fronte.

NOTE 57, p. 192.

GESCHICHTE der Kunst, part ii. p. 328. "He produced the Antigone, his first tragedy, in the third year of the seventy-seventh Olympiad." The time is tolerably exact, but it is quite a mistake to suppose that this first tragedy was the Antigone. Neither is it so called by Samuel Petit, whom Winkelmann quotes in a note. He expressly puts the Antigone in the third year of the eighty-fourth Olympiad. The following year, Sophocles went with Pericles to Samos, and the year of this expedition can be determined with exactness. In my life of Sophocles, I show, from a comparison with a passage of the elder Pliny, that the first tragedy of this author was probably Triptolemus. (Lib. xviii. sect. 12.) Pliny is speaking of the various excellence of the fruits of different countries, and concludes thus: "Hæ fuere sententiæ, Alexandro magno regnante, cum clarissima fuit Græcia, atque in toto terrarum orbe potentissima; ita tamen ut ante mortem ejus annis fere CXLV. Sophocles poeta in fabula Triptolemo frumentum Italicum ante cuncta laudaverit, ad verbum translata sententia:

> Et fortunatam Italiam frumento canere candido."

He is here not necessarily speaking of the first tragedy of Sophocles, to be sure. But the date of that, fixed by Plutarch, the scholiast, and the Arundelian marbles, as the seventy-seventh Olympiad, corresponds so exactly with the date assigned by Pliny to the Triptolemus, that we can hardly help regarding that as the first of Sophocles' tragedies. The calculation is easily made. Alexander died in the hundred and fourteenth Olympiad. One hundred and forty-five years cover thirty-six Olympiads and one year, which subtracted from the total, gives seventy-seven. The Triptolemus of Sophocles appeared in the seventy-seventh Olympiad; the last year of this same Olympiad is the date of his first tragedy: we may naturally conclude, therefore, that these tragedies are one. I show at the same time that Petit might have spared himself the writing of the whole half of the chapter in his "Miscellanea" which Winkelmann quotes (xviii. lib. iii.). In the passage of Pliny, which he thinks to amend, it is quite unnecessary to change the name of the Archon Aphepsion into Demotion, or ἀνεψιός. He need only have looked from the third to the fourth year of the seventy-seventh Olympiad to find that the Archon of that year was called Aphepsion by the ancient authors quite as often as Phædon, if not oftener. He is called Phædon by Diodorus Siculus, Dionysius Halicarnassus, and the anonymous author of the table of the Olympiads; while the Arundelian marbles, Apollodorus, and, quoting him, Diogenes Laertius, call him Aphepsion. Plutarch calls him by both names; Phædon in the life of Theseus and Aphepsion in the life of Cimon. It is therefore probable, as Palmerius supposes, "Aphepsionem et Phædonem Archontas fuisse eponymos; scilicet, uno in magistratu mortuo, suffectus fuit alter." (Exercit. p. 452.) This reminds me that Winkelmann, in his first work on the imitation of Greek art, allowed an error to creep in with regard to Sophocles. "The most beautiful of the youths danced naked in the theatre, and Sophocles, the great Sophocles, was in his youth the first to show himself thus to his fellow-citizens." Sophocles never danced naked on the stage. He danced around the trophies after the victory of Salamis, according to some authorities naked, but according to others clothed. (Athen. lib. i. p. m. 20.) Sophocles was one of the boys who was brought for safety to Salamis, and on this island it pleased the tragic muse to assemble her three favorites in a gradation typical of their future career. The bold Æschylus helped gain the victory; the blooming Sophocles danced around the trophies; and on the same happy island, on the very day of the victory, Euripides was born